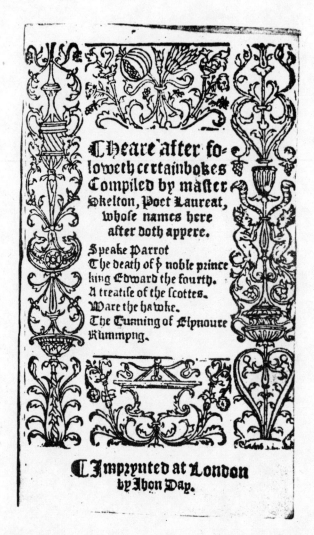

THE TITLE-PAGE OF THE EDITION OF 'CERTAIN BOOKS
COMPILED BY MASTER SKELTON,' PRINTED BY JOHN
DAY, c. 1565.

JOHN SKELTON

A Sketch of his Life and Writings

By L. J. Lloyd, M.A.

Sometime Scholar of Emmanuel College, Cambridge;
Lecturer in English in the University College
of the South West of England, Exeter

Basil Blackwell · Oxford · 1938

PREFACE

THIS little book does not claim to be anything more than an introduction to its subject. Work on Skelton continues on both sides of the Atlantic: discoveries will come. More will be known about his life, and many obscurities in the poems will be cleared away. Little however is likely to appear which will greatly enhance his reputation as a poet. That is, or should be, secure. In this belief I have attempted to suggest that Skelton is worth considerably more attention than has usually been given to him by readers of poetry, in the hope that they may be induced to discover for themselves what manner of man was the Rector of Diss.

I have been very greatly helped in the writing of this sketch, and many acknowledgments are made in the notes. But it is with especial gratitude that I thank Dr. G. G. Coulton, who for two years gave me access to his great store of learning and kindness; the Master and Fellows of Christ's College, Cambridge, who elected me to the Adelaide Stoll Research Studentship which made this work possible; the Master and Fellows of Emmanuel College, for innumerable kindnesses; many helpers at the Cambridge University Library, the libraries of Corpus Christi and Trinity, the British Museum, the Bodleian, the Public Record Office, and the Henry Huntingdon Library, California; Messrs. W. H. Robinson, Ltd., of Pall Mall, for permission to reproduce the title-page of the copy of Skelton in their possession; Mr. Reginald Horrox; Professor R. C. Bald; my wife, and Professor Lewis Horrox, who kindly took upon themselves the burden of proof-reading.

Finally, my warmest thanks are due to Mr. H. S. Bennett, who first suggested this study to me. Any merits it may have are very largely due to his encouragement, help and example, to which I am far more deeply indebted than I can say here.

L. J. LLOYD.

Exeter, August, 1938.

CONTENTS

CHAPTER I

EARLY YEARS

I

LYTTON STRACHEY once observed, writing of
Voltaire's tragedies, that the historian of literature
is little more than a historian of exploded reputations.
The singular difficulty, or perhaps good fortune, which
confronts the biographer of John Skelton is that the
subject of his memoir has at no time possessed any reputation, save for the appreciation of contemporaries, to
explode. After a career of meteoric brilliance and untiring
industry, the most colourful personality in the history of
English letters from Chaucer to Spenser suddenly disappeared into almost complete obscurity, to be ignored
or at best derided from thenceforth by everyone whose
business or delight it was to write about English literature. Consistently neglected or misunderstood, by the
eighteenth century he had been reduced to the level of a
buffoon. Alexander Pope, imitating the first epistle of the
second book of Horace in 1737, expresses the cultivated
opinion of his time:

> Chaucer's worst ribaldry is learn'd by rote,
> And beastly Skelton Heads of Houses quote,

and informs the reader further, in a note, that Skelton's
poetry consists 'almost wholly of Ribaldry, Obscenity,
and Billingsgate language.'

Yet at the height of his fortunes, in 1499 for example,
John Skelton had scarcely a peer among his contemporaries. He was a royal tutor, a churchman, a poet and
scholar of acknowledged reputation, a wit, a musician.
The King had given him a silken robe embroidered with
gold; three Universities had presented him with the
laurel crown; William Caxton had invited his assistance

and honoured his opinion in the matter of a translation of the Aeneid which he was bringing out, and Desiderius Erasmus of Rotterdam, overcome with admiration of his talents, had discerned that he was the British Homer.[1]

It is a far cry to Billingsgate from magnificence of this sort, and Skelton might well have complained with his own Edward IV:

> *Miseremini mihi*, ye that be my frendis,
> This world has formed me downe to fall.

It was not indeed until 1843 that Alexander Dyce published his great edition of the poems, and began a process of rehabilitation which is even now far from complete.

. . . . . .

The materials for a biography of Skelton are extremely scanty.[2] There is little documentary evidence, and what is known of him has largely to be gathered from what he says about himself, and from what admirers and others were moved to say about him from time to time. Happily he was at no time tempted to hide his light, and his own account of himself is still the most considerable piece of information which is to be had.

He was born, probably in Cumberland, but possibly in Norfolk, somewhere about 1460. Nothing is known of his parents. The name Skelton is a common one in the North of England, and of the thirty or so Skeltons who

---

[1] Grecia Meonio quantum debebat Homero
Mantua Virgilio
Tantum Skeltoni iam se debere fatetur
Terra Britanna suo.
Primus in hanc Latio deduxit ab orbe Camoenas,
Primus hic edocuit
Exculte pureque loqui. Te principe Skelton
Anglia nil metuat
Velcum Romanis versu certare poetis.
Vive valeque diu.
Preserved Smith: *Erasmus*, 1923. The complete text of the poem, *Carmen Extemporale*, is given pp. 453-4, and a translation p. 64.

[2] A. Dyce: *The Poetical Works of John Skelton*, 2 vols, 1843, I, v-lii; F. Brie, *Skelton Studien*, in *Englische Studien*, Band 37, pp. 1-36; J. M. Berdan, *Early Tudor Poetry*, 1920, pp. 92-5; R. L. Dunbabin, *Mod. Lang. Rev.*, vol. XII, 1917, pp. 129-39; A. Thümmel, *Stüdien über John Skelton*, 1905.

appear in the *Alumni Cantabrigienses*[1] six come from Cumberland and three from Yorkshire. Ten come from Lincoln or Norfolk, but it is reasonable to suppose that in some of these cases the spelling may be an error for Shelton, which is a Norfolk name. The birthplaces of the others are not known.

The association of John Skelton with Cumberland first appears in Fuller, in 1662:

> John Skelton was a younger branch of the Skeltons of Skelton in this county (Cumberland). I crave leave of the reader, hitherto not having full instructions and preserving the undoubted Title of this County unto him, to defer his character to Norfolk where he was Beneficed at Diss therein.[2]

Anthony à Wood records the same tradition again in 1691: 'John Skelton was originally, if not nearly, descended from the Skeltons of Cumberland.'[3]

Fuller also states the case for Norfolk:

> John Skelton is placed in this county on a double probability. First, because an ancient family of his name is eminently known long fixed therein. Secondly, because he was beneficed at Diss.

Skelton himself, in his *Lamentatio Urbis Norvicen*,[4] addresses the city:

> Ah decus, ah patriae specie pulcherrima dudum,

and Dyce suggested that 'patriae' may here be used in the sense of 'native county.' If it is there is no more to be said, but the possibility of such usage is at best doubtful.

On the whole the evidence for a northern origin for Skelton is far more convincing. One of his earliest poems is an elegy on the fourth Earl of Northumberland, who was murdered in a popular rising in 1489, and it is very possible that he was commissioned to write it. As will be seen, the poem contains a good deal of personal feeling.

---

[1] Ed. J. and J. A. Venn, 1922.
[2] *The Worthies of England*, p. 221.
[3] *Athenae Oxonienses*, I, p. 49.
[4] Dyce, I, p. 174.

Moreover, his virulent hatred of the Scots and his life-long preoccupation with their malignancies, together with his familiarity not only with northern topography but with northern language, seem difficult to account for in a man born of southern parents.

It is just possible however that his family migrated from Cumberland to Norfolk during the last quarter of the fifteenth century.[1]

One further theory remains to be noted. In 1908 Dr. R. L. Ramsay pointed out that there exist three references to a John Skelton in the *Household Book* of John, Duke of Norfolk, 1481–1490.[2] Under October 3rd, 1483, appears the entry:

> Item, the same day, paid to John a Godsalfe and to John Skelton for to buy them leverey gownys vi s viij d.

This John Skelton is mentioned again among those of the Duke's household who were attending him to London, and later as one of

> the M. men that my Lord hath graunted to the King.

The 'M. men' were the Duke's forces at Bosworth, where he lost his life: the names of the contingent are listed under towns, and John Skelton comes from Reigate in Surrey. It is almost impossible however to believe that these entries refer to the poet. In the first place Skelton himself says nothing of all this. Nowhere does he imply that he was ever the Duke's man, or that he appeared on Bosworth field, and it cannot be doubted

---

[1] I had reached the above conclusion when I read Mr. H. L. R. Edwards' valuable genealogical study in *The Review of English Studies*, vol. II, 1935, pp. 406–20. Mr. Edwards has examined, together with much other material, the records of the chief branch of the Skeltons, whose seat was Armathwaite Castle, and who had established their hold in Cumberland through assiduous loyalty to the King. To get their land they seem to have migrated south, and on returning to have left several members who preferred the life in and around London. One Edward Skelton (perhaps the poet's father) had been sergeant-at-arms to Henry VI 'at least as early as 1452.' The annuity grant made to him in 1486 is to 'Edward Skelton, Knight.'

[2] R. L. Ramsay, *Magnyfycence*, E.E.T.S. repr. 1925, cxxvii.

4

that if he had been a soldier somebody would have been reminded of the fact. To Skelton everything that had ever happened to him was good literary material. Moreover, the Skelton of the *Household Book* seems to have been a comparatively unimportant person. It is hardly likely that the man who, in 1490, is reverentially saluted by William Caxton as a finished scholar and a recent laureate of the University of Oxford, would be receiving 3s. 4d. for a new livery in 1483. The spectacle of such a man fighting at Bosworth is even more difficult to imagine. It is in fact more than likely that in 1485 Skelton was in Cambridge, about to proceed to his Master's degree, and it is hard to see how in the circumstances he could have found time to wear the Duke of Norfolk's livery and move about the country with his patron.

II

Of Skelton's schooldays nothing is known, but that his university was Cambridge he says himself:

> Alma parens O Cantabrigiensis
> . . . tibi quondam carus alumnus eram.[1]

His college was probably what is now Peterhouse, where his friend William Rukshaw was a Fellow.[2] In the *Alumni Cantabrigienses* Skelton appears as 'perhaps B.A. 1478–9,' and this suggestion is satisfactory from every point of view. The education which he obtained at Cambridge lay well within ordinary scholastic tradition, for his undergraduate life was passed at a time when the university was still practically untouched by Humanism, and the old studies, though nearing the end of their glory, still held the field. To the end of his life Skelton firmly believed that Latin is the only sure basis of sound and accurate scholarship. The magnificent structure of Latin learning, raised by the expenditure of so much toil

[1] *A Replycacion*, etc., Dyce I, p. 207.
[2] Dyce, I, p. 14. *Tetrastichon Skelton. Laureati ad Magistrum Rukshaw.*

5

and genius, seemed to him, as it did to countless others, well-nigh indestructible, even eternal. The Truth was known, and it had been arranged within orderly and well-defined limits for the benefit of those who wished to learn of it for themselves. Everything had been said, and well said, in Latin, from the lyrics of Catullus to the Office of the Mass. The true scholar was he who could use this great heritage as his own, and a Master of Arts of the University of Cambridge was the servant of no man.

It is to his infinite credit that when in later years Greek studies suddenly burst upon the academic world Skelton attempted to keep an open mind and examine the new situation calmly and fairly. But he was a Latinist to the backbone, and he found it hard work.

In these early years at Cambridge he worked hard, and read widely both in Latin and English, taking all knowledge for his province, and rapidly gaining a reputation as a fine scholar. Modern criticism has been unkind to what remains of his Latin, but his contemporaries thought very highly of his talents and rewarded them in suitable fashion. It would at any rate be difficult to imagine a more glowing testimonial than this passage from Caxton's preface to *The Boke of Eneydos*, which came out in 1490:

> . . . But I praye mayster John Skelton, late created poete laureate in the vnyuersite of oxenforde, to ouersee and correcte this sayd booke, And taddresse and expowne where as shalle be founde faulte to theym that shall requyre it. For hym I knowe for suffycyent to expowne and englysshe euery dyffyculte that is therin. For he hath late translated the epystlys of Tulle, and the boke of dyodorus syculus, and diuerse other werkes oute of latyn in to englysshe, not in rude and olde langage, but in polysshed and ornate terms craftely, as he that hath redde vyrgyle, ouyde, tullye, and all the other noble poetes and oratours to me vnknowen: And also he hath redde the ix muses and vnderstande theyr

6

musicalle scyences, and to whom of theym eche scyence is appropred. I suppose he hath dronken of Elycons well.[1]

The importance of this document cannot be over-stressed. It proves conclusively that at the age of thirty John Skelton had arrived. He is a finished scholar, and his name is evidently common property among the learned—already he has a crowd of distinctions at his back. He is not only a profound Latinist: he can also write beautiful English. He can employ polished and ornate terms; he is in other words in command of all those intricacies and subtleties of expression without which no writer of English in the fifteenth century could hope to gain distinction. Caxton, a writer himself, is overcome by humility: he says everything he can. The country of the nine muses is certainly a large field, but Skelton is to speak for himself of history, the drama, poetry, music and astronomy. What he knew of other things, dancing for example, may perhaps be left to conjecture and to Caxton's wondering admiration.

Exactly when Skelton gained the distinction of laureate has, so far, not been discovered: it would be very useful to know the precise value of Caxton's 'late.' No records remain which give a correct list of the honours awarded at Oxford during this period. To Skelton his laureation was perhaps the most important event of his life, and it often served him as a shield against envy and rancour in later years. The laurel crown was given for proficiency in the composition of Latin verse, for evidence of a thorough acquaintance with the rules of grammar, rhetoric and the whole very complicated art of versification; and though it was a purely academic distinction and had nothing to do with the modern conception of an official, national poet, it was nevertheless one of the most distinguished favours which it was possible for an academic society to award. Skelton referred to it immediately whenever his abilities were questioned, during his

[1] Dyce, I, xi–xii.

7

literary quarrel with Sir Christopher Garnesche for example:

> What eylythe thé, rebawde, on me to raue?
> A kyng to me myn habyte gaue:
> At Oxforth, the vniversyte,
> Auaunsid I was to that degre;
> By hole consent of theyr senate,
> I was made poete lawreate.[1]

Mention is again made of it in *Why were ye Calliope?*

> Calliope,
> As ye may se,
> Regent is she
>   Of poetes al,
> Whiche gaue to me
> The high degre
> Laureat to be
>   Of fame royall;
> Whose name enrolde
> With silke and golde
> I dare be bolde
>   Thus for to were.[2]

The habit granted to him by Henry VII is not altogether easy to explain. It is difficult to see whether it was given in recognition of his laureation or whether it had some connection with the title 'orator regius' which Skelton occasionally used. There is no evidence of emoluments for services as official poet, but Skelton says himself that he composed poems by royal command, and there is nothing improbable in the suggestion that he was at times employed to prepare Latin verses for use on ceremonial occasions. At any rate he wore the Tudor colours, white and green, as appears from the poems against Garnesche:

> Your sworde ye swere, I wene,
> So tranchaunt and so kene,
> Xall kyt both wyght and grene:

[1] Dyce, I, p. 128, ll. 79–84.
[2] Dyce, I, p. 197, ll. 1–11.

8

> Your foly ys to grett
> The kynges colours to threte. . . .[1]

and it is possible that both dress and title had something to do with his position as royal tutor, for during his term of office he wrote at least one manual for the edification of his pupil:

> The Duke of Yorkis creauncer whan Skelton was,
>   Now Henry the viij. Kyng of Englonde,
> A tratyse he deuysid and browght it to pas,
>   Called *Speculum Principis*, to bere in his honde,
>   Therin to rede, and to vnderstonde
> All the demenour of princely astate,
> To be our Kyng, of God preordinate; . . . .[2]

'Orator regius' is no fanciful title for such an author, and Skelton would not think any the worse of it for being, as it possibly was, self-styled.[3]

He became tutor to Prince Henry somewhere about 1494–5, for he states distinctly that he taught his pupil the rudiments, and in 1499, when Erasmus met them both at Eltham, Henry was nine years old.[4] His sister Mary had her first tutor when she was five. Skelton is perfectly clear on the matter:

> The honor of Englond I lernyd to spelle,
> In dygnyte roialle that doth excelle:
> Note and marke wyl thys parcele;
> I yaue hym drynke of the sugryd welle
> Of Eliconys waters crystallyne,
> Aqueintyng hym with the Musys nyne.
> Yt commyth the wele me to remorde,
> That creaunser was to thy sofre (yne) lorde:

---

[1] Dyce, I, p. 124, ll. 138–142.

[2] *The Garlande of Laurell*, Dyce, I, pp. 410–11, ll. 1226–32.

[3] But see H. L. R. Edwards and William Nelson, *P.M.L.A.*, Vol. LIII, June, 1938, pp. 601–3, 611, for the view that the title was given to Skelton in May 1512 by Henry VIII.

[4] The immediate outcome of the visit of Erasmus to Eltham was a poem *Prosopopaeia Britanniae Majoris*, which was printed in the first edition of the *Adagia* in 1500. Prince Henry had appeared to Erasmus as 'having already something royal in his demeanour, in which loftiness of mind was combined with singular culture.'

9

JOHN SKELTON

> It plesyth that noble prince roialle
> Me as hys master for to calle
> In hys lernyng primordialle.[1]

It is perhaps significant that in 1493 Skelton, recently laureated by the University of Louvain, also received the laurel crown from his own university. The Grace runs:

> Sub Magistris Johanne Lownd et Ricardo Huddilston procuratoribus concesse anno domini Millesimo ccccxciij et anno Regni Regis Henrici vij ix conceditur Johanni Skelton Poete in partibus transmarinis atque Oxon laurea ornato ut apud nos eadem decoraretur.[2]

Thus he was at the height of his academic reputation when he was appointed tutor to Prince Henry. It is strange that he never alludes to his laureation by a foreign university: the only evidence that it was Louvain is contained in a poem written by Richard Whittington in praise of Skelton as late as 1519:

> In clarissimi Scheltonis Louvaniensis poetae laudes epigramma.[3]

There is no other record of Skelton's connection with Louvain: there is not even evidence that he was ever abroad. According to Rashdall[4] however, Louvain was a stronghold of anti-Reformation learning, and it is possible that admiration of Skelton's achievements, combined with approval of his unshakeable orthodoxy, may have moved the Senate of the university to do him honour. There is unfortunately no information concerning his laureation to be had from the Louvain registers.

It would be as idle as it would be fascinating to speculate as to the effect of Skelton's teaching on his royal pupil, though Agnes Strickland, it may be remembered, thought differently. 'How probable it is,' she remarks,

---

[1] *Against Garnesche*, Dyce, I, p. 129, ll. 95–105.
[2] *Grace Book B*, ed. Mary Bateson, Publications of the Cambridge Antiquarian Society, 1903; pp. 53–4.
[3] Dyce, I, xvi–xix.
[4] Hastings Rashdall, *The Universities of Europe in the Middle Ages*, 1895, II, pt. I, p. 263.

'that the corruption imparted by this ribald and ill-living wretch laid the foundation for his royal pupil's grossest crimes.'

It is certain however that Skelton had good material to work upon. Holbein's famous portraits of Henry at the age of fifty have obscured in most people's minds the simple fact that at his accession he was a singularly handsome and cultured young man, the most promising prince in Europe. The Venetian Ambassador, who, as Professor Berdan justly remarks, was only concerned with telling a plain tale plainly, thus expresses his opinion:

In this Eighth Henry, God combined such corporal and mental beauty, as not merely to surprise but to astound all men. Who could fail to be struck with admiration on perceiving the lofty position of so glorious a prince to be in such accordance with his stature, giving manifest proof of that intrinsic mental superiority which is inherent in him? His face is angelic rather than handsome: his head imperial (*Cesarina*) and bald, and he wears a beard, contrary to English custom. Who would not be amazed when contemplating such singular corporal beauty, coupled with such bold address, adapting itself with the greatest ease to every manly exercise. He sits his horse well, and manages him yet better; he jousts and wields his spear, throws the quoit, and draws the bow, admirably; plays at tennis most dexterously; and nature having endowed him in youth with such gifts, he was not slow to enhance, preserve and augment them with all industry and labour. It seeming to him monstrous for a prince not to cultivate moral and intellectual excellence, so from childhood he applied himself to grammatical studies, and then to philosophy and holy writ, thus obtaining the reputation of a lettered and excellent Prince. Besides the Latin and his native tongue, he learned Spanish, French, and Italian. He is kind and affable, full of graciousness and courtesy, and liberal; particularly so to men of science (*virtuosi*), whom he is never weary of obliging.[1]

The same enthusiasm appears in a letter to Erasmus from his former pupil Lord Mountjoy:

[1] Berdan, *op. cit.*, p. 45.

JOHN SKELTON

What, my dear Erasmus, may you not look for from a prince, whose great qualities no one knows better than yourself, and who not only is no stranger to you, but esteems you so highly! He has written to you, as you will perceive, under his own hand, an honour which falls but to few. Could you but see how nobly he is bearing himself, how wise he is, his love for all that is good and right, and especially his love for men of learning, you would need no wings to fly into the light of this new risen and salutary star. Oh, Erasmus, could you but witness the universal joy, could you but see how proud our people are of their new sovereign, you would weep for pleasure. Heaven smiles, earth triumphs, and flows with milk and honey and nectar. This king of ours is no seeker after gold, or gems, or mines of silver. He desires only the fame of virtue and eternal life. I was lately in his presence. He said that he regretted that he was still so ignorant; I told him that the nation did not want him to be himself learned, the nation wanted him only to encourage learning. He replied that without knowledge life would not be worth our having.[1]

It would be manifestly unfair to deny Skelton at least something of the credit for this round of accomplishments. He cannot have failed to be a stimulating teacher, enthusiastic and skilful: again and again Henry's mind must have caught fire from such a man. No doubt Skelton's appointment was mainly due to his reputation as a Latinist, but no careful reader can doubt that they played music together, and there is nothing fanciful in the suggestion that Skelton encouraged his pupil to explore the literature of his own country, to read the works of the great Triumvirate, Chaucer, Lydgate, and Gower.

It is clear from Caxton's preface that Skelton was an enthusiastic student of English, but even if the preface did not exist there could be no doubt in the matter, for Skelton himself, in *Phyllyp Sparowe*, enumerates and describes the English books he has read.[2] He makes a long list, and it covers a wide range. It includes Chaucer,

[1] J. A. Froude, *The Life and Letters of Erasmus*, ed. 1900, pp. 96–97. See also P. S. Allen, *Opus Epistolarum Des. Erasmi Roterodami*, 1906, letter 215.
[2] Dyce, I, p. 70, ll. 634–683.

the Arthurian cycle, the adventures of the four sons of
Aymon, and the stories of Judas Maccabaeus, Julius
Caesar, and Hannibal. The 'matter of Troy' is there, and
the résumé includes Ulysses, Penelope, Ahasuerus,
Esther, Alexander the Great and Lars Porsena, all in
English dress. To these are to be added the chronicles,
ballads, songs and fabliaux which were common property
in the fifteenth century.

Of far greater interest to the modern reader however is
what Skelton has to say about Chaucer, Lydgate and
Gower, and it will be well to quote the passage in full:

> Gowers Englysh is olde,
> And of no value told;
> His mater is worth gold,
> And worthy to be enrold.
> In Chauser I am sped,
> His tales I haue red:
> His mater is delectable,
> Solacious and commendable;
> His Englysh well alowed,
> So as it is enprowed,
> For as it is enployd,
> There is no Englysh voyd,
> At those dayes moch commended,
> And now men wold haue amended
> His Englysh, whereat they barke,
> And mar all they warke:
> Chaucer, that famus clerke,
> His termes were not darke,
> But plesaunt, easy, and playne;
> No worde he wrote in vayne.
> Also Johnn Lydgate
> Wryteth after an hyer rate;
> It is dyffuse to fynde
> The sentence of his mynde,
> Yet wryteth he in his kynd,
> No man that can amend
> Those maters that he hath pende;
> Yet some men fynde a faute,
> And say he wryteth to haute.[1]

[1]Dyce, I, p. 75, ll. 784-818.

JOHN SKELTON

This at first sight seems to be nothing but a dutiful echo of the contemporary critical position. Gower's English is useless as a model, though it is full of matter. Chaucer writes in easy and polished English, and is also a mine of delectable information. But Lydgate writes 'after a higher rate,' since it is often difficult to see precisely what he means. He has become so recondite as to be positively obscure: he has possessed himself of that pearl of mediaeval wisdom, *subtilitas*.

Skelton however was a better critic than his contemporaries. It is obvious that the greater part of his disquisition is mere lip-service. There can be no doubt that he admired Lydgate and by no means despised *subtilitas*, but it is Chaucer for whom his real enthusiasm is reserved.[1] The conventional tribute is paid to both Gower and Lydgate, but no mention of their works is made in the poem. Moreover even into the praise of Lydgate Skelton inserts a phrase which hitherto seems to have been overlooked:

> Yet wryteth he *in his kynd*,
> No man that can amend
> Those matters that he hath pende.

He is willing enough, that is, to admit that Lydgate has no rival in his own sphere, but he is far from declaring that Lydgate's 'kynd' is the best kind of poetry.

The tribute to Chaucer is very different, for Skelton shows that he has read him:

> . . . Palamon and Arcet
> Duke Theseus and Partelet;
> And of the Wyfe of Bath,
> That worketh much scath
> Whan her tale is told.

[1] Hoccleve was the first panegyrist of Chaucer's memory, and Lydgate the most influential of Hoccleve's followers, among whom are Dunbar and Caxton. In hardly a single instance however is stress laid upon Chaucer's real merits: the fifteenth century was unable to perceive his superiority over poets like Gower and Lydgate. See Berdan, *op. cit.*, Chap. III, and Dunbar, Poems, ed. Small, 1893, p. 10.

EARLY YEARS

> . . . And of the loue so hote
> That made Troylus to dote
> Vpon fayre Cressyde,
> And what they wrote and sayd.

If he publicly admires Gower and Lydgate it is chiefly because it would seem strange if he did not. There is more to add however. The three poets appear again in *The Garlande of Laurell*, written when Skelton was over sixty. Chaucer, Gower and Lydgate welcome him into their company, and in reply to their greetings he addresses a compliment to each of them in turn. Of the work of Gower and Lydgate he says nothing, but Chaucer moves him to an outburst of admiration:

> O noble Chaucer, whos pullisshyd eloquence
> Oure Englysshe rude so fresshely hath set out
> That bounde are we with all deu reuerence,
> With all oure strength that we can brynge about,
> To owe to yow our seruyce, and more if we mowte![1]

It could hardly have been otherwise, and it would not only have been disappointing but surprising if Skelton had not singled out Chaucer for special admiration and reverence. The author of *The Canterbury Tales* was a man after his own heart, and it may be that he recognized his kinship with him somewhat more clearly than we have a mind to do in these days. A man like Skelton must have seen at once the impassable gulf which lay between the stories, 'some sad, some mery,' of the Knight, the Pardoner, the Miller and the rest, and the earnest and respectable catalogues which Lydgate delighted to compile. Skelton cannot be blamed for his partial adherence to contemporary opinion, but one is grateful that he said what he really thought.

In *The Garlande of Laurell* there is mentioned a work now lost, a *New Gramer in Englysshe compylyd*. It must have been either an English grammar or a Latin grammar with explanations in English: it is pleasant to believe that it

[1] Dyce, I, p. 378, ll. 421-5.

15

was the former. Skelton always had the future of the language at heart, and he may have attempted to systematize his knowledge for Prince Henry's edification, for he was profoundly dissatisfied with the state of the language in his own day. Things seemed to him to be at a standstill. He complains bitterly in *Phyllyp Sparowe* that English is almost useless for any sort of coherent expression:

> Our naturall tong is rude,
> And hard to be enneude
> With pullysshed termes lusty;
> Our language is so rusty,
> So cankered, and so full
> Of frowardes, and so dull,
> That if I wolde apply
> To wryte ornatly,
> I wot not where to fynd
> Termes to serue my mynde.
>
> ll. 774–782.

Caxton, it will be remembered, found the same difficulty:

> And thus bytwene playn rude and curyous, I stande abasshed, but in my Judgemente the comyn termes that be dayli vsed, ben lyghter to be vnderstonde than the olde and auncyent englysshe.[1]

As Professor Berdan points out, there even seems to have been a tendency towards modernization of the earlier writers. The statement of Barclay:

> Right honorable Master ye me required late,
> A lovers confession abridging to amend
> And from corrupte Englishe in better to translate,[2]

may refer to Gower, but Skelton is quite explicit in his remarks on Chaucer:

> And now men wold haue amended
> His Englysh, whereat they barke,
> And mar all they warke.

He himself will have none of it, though the position was

[1] Berdan, *op. cit.*, p. 53. The passage is from Caxton's preface to his *Boke of Eneydos*.
[2] Berdan, *op. cit.*, p. 54.

16

certainly an unhappy one. There was no true realization of Chaucer's great merits: the secret of his versification had already been lost. Professor Pollard shows that many lines in Caxton's editions of *The Canterbury Tales* have, as they are printed, 'entirely ceased to be decasyllabics; they can be read in no other way than as trotting verses of four accents apiece.'[1] William Salesbury remarks in 1547:

> Similarly e final in English words is melted away for the most part, from the end of every word in pronunciation.

It is no wonder therefore that Skelton finds occasion to bewail the lack of literary models. It is fortunate for us and for his own reputation that he decided in the end to take the law into his own hands. He saw clearly that nothing new was likely to come out of Lydgate and the aureate and polished school, and he turned boldly towards the exploitation of an entirely novel kind of versification. The curious thing is however that to the end of his life he remained in great measure loyal to the old traditional models. He never for instance dissociated in his own mind the use of rhyme-royal from a formal and dignified occasion. What was almost his last poem was written in it, for ' the noble Countess of Surrey' could not be expected to look with any favour upon Skeltonics. His less formal metre does indeed put in an appearance, but in the daintiest fashion imaginable.

His fondness for allegory, moreover, never left him for long at a time, and he is not by any means at pains to alter or adapt the traditional framework, though he does more with it than any other writer since Chaucer. He is content to be stereotyped up to a point, but he preserves his freedom of action within the conventional bounds. There were, it must be noticed, two distinct personalities in John Skelton, the academic and the revolutionary, and one is never sure which of the two will suddenly come uppermost. It is even more doubtful which of the two Skeltons he himself really preferred.

[1] Berdan, *op. cit.*, p. 51. The passage is from Professor Pollard's edition of *The Castell of Labour*, Roxburgh Club, xl–xli.

CHAPTER II

THE RECTOR OF DISS

SKELTON'S appointment as royal tutor was the greatest honour that ever came to him, and except for an entertainment in his honour at Cambridge in 1495, it was almost the last.

The period of his greatest prosperity was nearly over, and the known facts of his life now become even fewer than before. He became a priest in 1498, and from the evidence of Erasmus, who met him at Eltham, it is clear that he was still Prince Henry's tutor in the summer of 1499. But from that time until 1504, when he appears as Rector of Diss in Norfolk, practically nothing is known of him, and there are few literary problems more fascinating than the question of what he did with those five years. The rectory of Diss was worth about £500 a year in modern currency: Skelton was in no danger of poverty. But it was obscure, ninety miles from London, and no sort of fitting reward for a man who had been a royal tutor and the most distinguished scholar of his generation. In no sense of the word could it be described as preferment.

Why, then, was he banished to Norfolk? There are two possible explanations open to the biographer. Skelton may have been dismissed from his post for misbehaviour, or he may himself have asked for the living. In 1502 there appears an entry in 'Actes, Orders, and Decrees made by the King and his Counsell, remaining amongst the records of the Court, now commonly called the Court of Requests' which may possibly throw some light on the problem:

> 10 Junii apud Westminster Jo. Skelton commissus carceribus Janitoris Domini Regis.[1]

If this entry refers to the poet everything seems to be

---

[1] Dyce, I, xxvi.

explained, but nothing more than the bare record remains.
It would serve very well as the basis for a hypothesis, if
Skelton's violent and irascible nature is taken into account.
A quarrel, perhaps with the young and ambitious Wolsey,
or a piece of insolence at Court, is followed by a slight
term of imprisonment, and afterwards, in consideration
for past services, banishment to an obscure and far from
lucrative country rectory. This explanation has a good
deal of probability to recommend it, for Skelton's fierce
temper can hardly fail to have placed him in many other
awkward situations, which have no memorial. That, however, is the most that can be said in the absence of further
evidence. A good deal on the other hand may be said for
the point of view that the rectory of Diss was his own
deliberate choice. It is obvious that when he came to write
The Bowge of Courte he had lost any illusions he may once
have possessed about the advantages and delights of life
at Court, and about the ultimate fate of such as put their
trust in princes. He may well have desired above all
things to be out of it. *The Bowge of Courte* is an obvious if
not particularized satire, and it is unlikely that its general
thesis is part of a mere literary exercise. A connection
between the poem and its author's retirement from
Court to the country is at any rate extremely plausible.
Literary ambition may also have had something to do
with his decision: Norfolk would at least be quiet. It
must have been well nigh impossible to write easily at
Court, in the midst of continual jealousy and rancour,
and Skelton was always quarrelling. It seems almost as if
his nature required this particular stimulus. If he could
not quarrel with a single enemy he quarrelled with a
group: if there was no hostile group to be had he
quarrelled with a system. Disagreement of some kind can
be found in almost every poem he wrote, and this mili-
tancy broke him in the end. Another consideration enters
at this point. If it could be shown that Skelton himself
elected to go to Diss, the evidence for a Norfolk birth-

19

place would become much more convincing than it has
been up to the present. It is easy to see Skelton looking
forward eagerly, now that his appointment as Henry's
tutor has come to an end, to a quiet retirement among
admiring and congenial friends, in the midst of a countryside that he knows and loves, and had explored as a boy.
This is all plausible enough, though there is woefully
little behind it. At all events it makes a better show than
the theory of incarceration and banishment, which has
only an isolated and unsupported statement to recommend it. Diss evidently remained Skelton's home until
1511 at least, though he left it from time to time, on
visits to London.[1] Never at any time does he complain
of his circumstances: we do not even hear a Chaucerian
complaint to his purse. Skelton, for all his turbulence,
gives one the impression of being one of those rare
spirits to whom the goods of this world matter very
little. He was probably as happy at Diss as he would have
been anywhere else, and though he was one of those who
try their friends very hard there is evidence to show
that he was by no means without them. His life at Diss
moreover was not without incident. Whatever may be
thought of the 'merie Tales of Maister Skelton, very
pleasaunt for the recreacion of the minde,'[2] which
came out after his death, with all their coarse and somewhat pointless buffoonery, it must be admitted that they
imply a tradition that the Rector of Diss was on good
terms with his parishioners and by no means averse from
a piece of horseplay. Skelton's latter-day reputation as a
merry-wit may not be wholly without foundation, and
there is the obviously first hand information of *Elynour
Rummynge* and a somewhat unfortunate 'epitaphe' on two
of these same parishioners[3] to give such a view ample

[1] See Edwards and Nelson, *loc. cit.*, pp. 611, 614–5, 620–1.
[2] First printed by Thomas Colwell 'beneath the Conduit at the signe of S.
John Evangelist', in an undated pamphlet. Dyce reprints the whole work, I,
lii–lxxxviii.
[3] Dyce, I, pp. 168–73.

20

support. The obscurity which surrounds his activities during his residence at Diss is made still more mysterious by various rumours and traditions which have survived from this time. He is supposed for example to have carried on a feud against the Dominicans, and at their instigation to have been called to account by his Bishop for keeping a mistress. Bale is the authority for this story, and he tells it with conviction:

> Cum quibusdam blateronibus fraterculis praecipue Dominicanis bellum gerebat continuum. Sub pseudopontifice Nordouicensi Ricardo Nixo, mulieram illam, quam sibi secreto ob Antichristi metum desponsauerat, sub concubinae titulo custodiebat, etc.[1]

The story appears, with very little alteration, in the subsequent accounts of Pits, Fuller and Anthony à Wood, and there can be no doubt that it was common property soon after Skelton's death. There is no documentary evidence, and it is impossible to accept a recent explanation of the problem. In 1913 Dr. Se Boyar noticed that in a visitation, by Skelton's Bishop Nix, or Nikke, of Norwich Cathedral in 1526, a certain 'Dominus Johannes Skelton' was accused of

> gravia crimina et nephanda peccata,

and Professor Berdan[2] is inclined to identify this Skelton with the poet, as it was through Nix that the trouble is traditionally supposed to have arisen. There is however a good deal of definite evidence against such a supposition. This John Skelton held in the first place a definite office in the Cathedral: he was 'camerarius et eleemosinarius,' and six years before he had in this capacity reported to his Bishop:

> quod omnia bene praeter quod pascuntur oves infra clausurum juxta claustrum.

Moreover, as a result of the 'gravia crimina' mentioned in the indictment he was sent to the dependent foundation

---

[1] Dyce, I, xxvii–xxix.
[2] *Op. cit.*, p. 204.

at Yarmouth, where apparently he died, for nothing
further is heard of him in connection with Norwich.[1]
In face of this strong tradition however it seems likely
that at some time during his residence at Diss Skelton
was accused of immorality, not perhaps for keeping a
mistress, but, what was far worse, making her his wife.
Bale, as has been seen, is quite clear on this important
point.

By this woman Skelton is said to have had several
children, and to have maintained on his death-bed that he
had always regarded her as his wife, but that to his
shame he had been too cowardly to admit the relationship.
There is an amusing and characteristic story in the *Merie
Tales* in which Skelton proudly holds up one of his
children before the astonished congregation and addresses
them as follows:

> You haue complayned of mee to the bysop that I doo
> keepe a fayre wench in my house: I dooe tell you, if you had
> any fayre wiues, it were some what to helpe me at neede;
> I am a man as you be: you haue foule wyues, and I haue a
> faire wenche, of the whyche I haue begotten a fayre boye, as
> I doe thinke, and as you all shall see. Thou wyfe, sayde
> Skelton, that hast my childe, be not afraid; bring me hither
> my childe to me: the whyche was doone. And he, shewynge
> his childe naked to all the parishe, sayde, How saye you,
> neibours all? is not this childe as fayre as is the beste of all
> yours? It hathe nose, eyes, handes, and feete, as well as any
> of your: it is not lyke a pygge, nor a calfe, nor like no foule
> nor no monstruous beast. If I had, sayde Skelton, broughte
> forthe thys chylde without armes or legges, or that it wer
> deformed, being a monstruous thyng, I woulde neuer haue
> blamed you to haue complayned to the bishop of me; but to
> complain without a cause, I say, as I said before in my an-
> tethem, *vos estis*, you be, and haue be, & wyll and shall be
> knaues, to complayne of me wythout a cause resonable.[2]

One is tempted to believe the whole story without

[1] I am indebted to Dr. G. G. Coulton for pointing this out to me.
[2] Dyce, I, lxi.

further comment: the scene is so exactly typical of at least one side of Skelton's strange and complex personality.

The obscurity of his country rectory however did not prevent him from keeping in touch with contemporary affairs in Church and State: his energy was not only undiminished but actually seemed to increase with the passage of years.

It cannot be doubted that he firmly made up his mind soon after his retirement that the task to which he would devote his life was that of criticism; criticism not only of the political or ecclesiastical situation but of every ill to which the land was subject, and during the course of his life he found much of which to complain. He became a fierce and unsparing critic, jealous and sensitive in the highest degree, and though he began innocuously enough, and was often diverted from his main purpose by the tempting claims of purely literary enterprise, his ideas gradually hardened, and he began to fix his gaze more and more steadfastly upon Wolsey, and to identify him with the rampant corruption among the clergy and the corresponding laxity on the part of the layman. Once he had firmly established this conviction in his mind, he expended every resource he possessed in a frenzied effort to make the offender's guilt plain to all the world. It is possible, as has been suggested, that the origin of the quarrel was a personal matter, though the fact need not lead one to question the purity of Skelton's motives. His passionate attachment to a church which he saw almost entirely discredited, and his devotion to a country which seemed to be falling into irreparable chaos, are more than sufficient to account for his hatred of the man who, as he thought, was responsible for the situation. Wolsey does not seem to have taken any immediate action, though he was not a man to rest quietly in the face of opposition: it will be remembered that he bought up every available copy of the anonymous *Rede me and be nott wrothe*. Skelton, moreover, was no ordinary pamphleteer, and the vigour and purpose of his writing were too strong to allow him to remain safe from molestation. Copies of the satires were undoubtedly passed from hand to hand, and they became in the end a menace which even Wolsey could not afford to ignore. Precisely at what time his patience finally became exhausted it is impossible to say, but it is certain that Skelton fled somewhere about 1523 to sanctuary at Westminster and the company of his friend Abbot Islip, in order to escape the officers whom Wolsey had sent out to apprehend him. From this time little more is heard of him until his death,[1] except that it is possibly he who appears, and then for the last time, in the Churchwardens Accounts of the neighbouring church of St. Margaret:

1529 Item, of Mr. Skelton for viii tapers: 2s. 8d.

It is pleasant and fitting to take our leave of him as he stands in the church, lighting his tapers. He died in this year on June 21st and was buried in the Chancel of St. Margaret's. His monument, which Bale says was of alabaster,[2] exhibited the short epitaph:

Johannes Skeltonus, vates Pierius, hic situs est.[3]

It is said that before he died he uttered, militant to the last, a prophecy concerning the downfall of Wolsey.

[1] Mr. Nelson, *P.M.L.A.*, Vol. LI, June 1936, pp. 393–8, and Vol. LIII, June 1938, pp. 620–1, maintains the view that Skelton eventually made his peace with Wolsey, who became his patron, and that his last six years were lived in freedom. There is tradition to be reckoned with, however, to say nothing of Skelton's independent character. Moreover, it is difficult to believe that Wolsey, of all people, could forgive and patronize the author of *Why come ye nat to Courte?* Even if the complimentary references to Wolsey attached to *The Garlande of Laurell*, *Howe the douty Duke of Albany*, and *A Replycacion*, are genuine, they prove nothing more than the fact that Skelton, growing less courageous with age, tried at various times to obtain his freedom. There is no positive evidence that he was successful, and it is certainly surprising, when what is known of his nature is considered, to find that he could bring himself to surrender.

[2] 'alabastrica.' By the kindness of the Librarian of the Bodleian I was allowed to see Bale's autograph MS.

[3] Skelton may have written it himself, for he is known to have composed epitaphs, at Islip's request, for some of the Westminster tombs.

CHAPTER III

EARLY POEMS

IT is impossible to say exactly when Skelton began to write, though there is a considerable amount of what is obviously prentice work still in existence. The earliest poem to which a date can reasonably be put is an elegy on Edward IV, who died in 1483, but it is almost certain that Skelton, industrious and facile as he was, had by this time written a good deal which is now lost. He seems to have begun his career as a poet, as Chaucer had begun more than a century before, by imitating the best models and by producing various sorts of pastiche before he was able to see clearly what his own line was to be.

The poems which remain from these early years are a curious mélange of dignified and academic versification, religious and philosophical reflection, satire, and buffoonery. On the whole they are of poor quality, but a careful examination of them reveals the promise of almost everything that Skelton was to do later, and it is impossible to mistake the authentic touch when it appears. It will be worth while to examine a few of these poems in some detail.

The elegy on Edward IV[1] has for its theme a mediaeval common-place,

Memento, Homo, quod cinis es et in cinerem reverteris,

and the poem is as common-place as the theme. The refrain, 'Et ecce nunc in pulvere dormio,' is reminiscent of Dunbar, who has treated much the same subject with infinitely more grace and assurance. Skelton is learned,

---

[1] Dyce, I, pp. 1–5. See Miss H. M. R. Murray: *The Middle English poem, Erthe upon Erthe*, E.E.T.S. 1911. This poem was very popular, and is often found in fifteenth-century MSS. Parts of it were sometimes inscribed on walls and tomb-stones.

Cf. Dunbar: *Memento, homo, quod cinis es*, Poems, ed. Small, p. 74.

sententious and academic. He writes correctly enough in the 'full-sailed rhyme-royal,' and with due appreciation of his authorities, but though a pleasant phrase occurs occasionally the poem as a whole never rises above the pedestrian, and there is not the slightest trace of personal feeling. The work is clearly an exercise, and the warning that Death spares neither king nor churl is made the excuse for an incongruous display of references to Absalom, Samson, Solomon, and Alexander the Great:

> Why should a man be proude or presume hye?
> Sainct Bernard therof nobly doth trete,
> Seyth a man is but a sacke of stercorry,
> And shall returne vnto wormis mete.
> Why, what cam of Alexander the greate?
> Or els of stronge Sampson, who can tell?
> Were not wormes ordeyned theyr flesh to frete?
> And of Salomon, that was of wit the well?
> Absolon profferyd his heare for to sell,
> Yet for al his bewte wormys ete him also;
> And I but late in honour dyd excel,
> *Et, ecce, nunc in pulvere dormio!*   ll. 73–84.

It is interesting, however, to see so early an example of Skelton's fondness for compiling catalogues.

Stereotyped elements are even more noticeable in another elegy,[1] on the fourth Earl of Northumberland who was murdered in 1489, but here they are combined with what seem to be traces of genuine feeling. The poem opens, very properly, with an invocation to the Muse of History:

> Of heuenly poems, O Clyo, calde by name
> In the colege of Musis goddes hystoriall,
> Adres thé to me, whiche am both halt and lame
> In elect vteraunce to make memoryall!
> To thé for souccour, to thé for helpe I call,
> Mine homely rudnes and dryghnes to expell
> With the freshe waters of Elyconys well.   ll. 8–14.

[1] Dyce, I, pp. 6–14.

Later on Skelton again apologizes for his impertinence in presuming to write at all, incompetent as he is:

> My wordes vnpullysht be, nakide and playne,
> Of aureat poems they want ellumynynge;

and says that his pen is 'rude,' 'enkankered all with rust.'

It is amusing to see Skelton, of all people, subscribing to this contemporary literary convention. No less humble man ever put pen to paper. But just as the Elizabethan poet was required to assure his readers that his poems were immortal, and the eighteenth-century writer to protest that he would never have published but for the importunity of his friends, so in the fifteenth century it was considered necessary to make a confession of incompetence. Alexander Barclay begs his readers, in the preface to his Eclogues,

> Not to be grieued with any playne sentence
> Rudely conuayed for lacke of eloquence,[1]

and Stephen Hawes describes his *Pastime of Pleasure* as

> Thys lytell boke oprest with rudenes
> Without rethorycke or colour crafty.[2]

Ralph Nevill too is extremely modest in his description of *The Castell of Pleasure*:

> Go humble style; submytte the to correcyon;
> Be not so bolde to presume to the presence
> Of ony but suche as be enuyronde with effecyon:
> Let them arrect theyr eeres to rebuke thy neglygence;
> To them thou perteynest of due congruence;
> Let them more curyously thy rurall termes affyle
> How thou sholdest be amended they haue best intellygence:
> Therfore submytte the to theym my poore and humble style.[3]

The greater part of the Northumberland Elegy is no less academic and derivative than this conceit. The 'vilane hastarddis' who murdered the Earl are certainly

---

[1] *The Eclogues of Alexander Barclay*, ed. Beatrice White, E.E.T.S. 1928, p. 3.
[2] *The Pastime of Pleasure*, ed. W. E. Mead, E.E.T.S., 1928, p. 5.
[3] *The Castell of Pleasure*, ed. Roberta D. Cornelius, E.E.T.S. 1930, p. 113.

blamed and reviled in fine rhetorical fashion, but Mars himself is also held responsible:

> O cruell Mars, thou dedly god of war!
> O dolorous tewisday, dedicate to thy name,
> When thou shoke thy sworde so noble a man to mar!
>
> ll. 113–115.

The Fates, too, are not forgotten:

> O Atropos, of the fatal sisters iii
> Goddes most cruel vnto the lyfe of man,
> All merciles, in the is no pite!   ll. 120–123.

At times indeed one seems to be listening to Bottom and his friends performing their most lamentable comedy of Pyramus and Thisbe. Towards the end of the poem, however, there is a note of personal feeling. Skelton addresses the young heir in terms which seem to betray real solicitude:

> O yonge lyon, but tender yet of age,
> Grow and encrese, remembre thyn estate:
> God thé assyst unto thyn herytage,
> And geue thé grace to be more fortunate!
>
> ll. 162–165.

The prayer which concludes the whole is full of dignity:

> O quene of mercy, O lady full of grace,
> Mayden most pure, and Goddes moder dere,
> To sorowful hartes chef comfort and solace,
> Of all women O flowre withouten pere!
> Pray to thy Son above the sterris clere,
> He to vouchesaf, by thy mediacion,
> To pardon thy seruaunt, and brynge to saluacion.
>
> ll. 204–210.

It is obvious that a man like Caxton would think a great deal of poems like these. They are correct and dignified, and written in rhyme-royal, the metre *par excellence* for poems treating of high matters. They make great use of the proper authorities, both Classical and Biblical, and they are full of 'polished and ornate terms.' They are, in short, the worthy results of patient study and careful attention to the traditional requirements of courtly verse.

A still greater number of polished and ornate terms appear in a group of four poems, printed by Richard Pynson, in a pamphlet which is unfortunately undated. These poems: *The auncient acquaintance, madam, betwen vs twayn, Knolege, aquayntance, resort, fauour with grace, Though ye suppose all jeperdys ar paste,* and *Go, pytyous hart, rasyd with dedly wo,*[1] are entirely traditional in form and content, though this is not the whole matter. The poet apparently addresses his mistress, a married woman with whom he had been in love, but there is little continuity between the four poems, and there is certainly no definite theme to be extracted from them. The frequent allusions and warnings in *The auncient acquaintance* seem however to imply personal experience of some kind. The other three poems may be simply poetic exercises, though *Knolege, aquayntance, resort* impresses the reader by its conviction. *Go, pytyous hart* is certainly modelled on Chaucer, and *Though ye suppose* is little more than a lengthy paraphrase of two lines of Virgil. But the most severe critic of fine writing could not but admire the 'craftiness' of these poems. Skelton loads every rift with ore, and epithet is piled upon epithet, allusion upon allusion. Alliteration is frequent: the array of polished terms is positively bewildering. The contemporary poetic vocabulary is ransacked to provide a very rich and strange confection:

> The topas rych and precyouse in vertew;
> Your ruddys wyth ruddy rubys may compare;
> Saphyre of sadness, enuayned wyth indy blew;
> The pullyshed perle youre whytenes doth declare;
> Dyamand poyntyd to rase oute hartly care;
> Gayne surfetous suspecte the emeraud comendable;
> Relucent smaragd, obiecte imcomperable; . . . .
>
> *Knolege, aquayntance,* ll. 15–21.

One almost begins to share Caxton's enthusiasm; surely

[1] Dyce, I, pp. 23–7.

29

this is the very perfection of writing. Skelton's skill and resource are astonishing, but, even so, it is with a shock of pleasurable surprise that one comes upon the last stanza of 'Knolege, aquayntance, resort,' for it is here that for the first time he breaks through his clinging web of verbiage and rises to something approaching his full stature:

Nothynge yerthly to me more desyrous
    Than to beholde youre bewteouse countenaunce:
But, hatefull absens, to me so enuyous,
    Though thou withdraw me from her by long dystaunce,
    Yet shall she neuer oute of remembraunce;
For I haue grauyd her wythin the secret wall
Of my trew hart, to loue her best of all!

ll. 43–49.

It is a surprising conclusion; dignified, balanced and weighty; the final couplet would not disgrace a Shakespeare sonnet. Certainly only a few English poets before Shakespeare can show anything better. Other occasional phrases, on a lower level of achievement, show something of Skelton's true quality; for instance:

Radyent Esperus, star of the clowdy nyght,
    Lode star to lyght these louers to theyr porte, ...

ll. 24–25.

To make extravagant claims for such very occasional felicities would be misleading, but they at least prove beyond a shadow of a doubt that their author was a poet. Salvation, one may admit, was not to come by way of polished and ornate terms, and it is fortunate that Skelton soon found other matters to occupy his attention. But when all is said of Lydgatian imitation and the Chaucerians it cannot but be admitted that the old material, though by now almost outworn, was still capable of producing music. Skelton at all events shows what can be done with it, and it never lost its fascination for him.

    Two characteristically satirical poems also survive

from these early years; *Womanhod, wanton, ye want*,[1] and
Agaynste a comely coystrowne. The first of these is a lover's
address to his mistress, and is bitter and vigorous in
tone. The poet complains that his mistress has no further
use for him now that his purse is empty:

> Why so koy and full of skorne?
> Myne horse is sold, I wene, you say: . . . .
>
> ll. 8–9.

He contents himself with railing, and with the warning
that she may yet be glad of him:

> For all your draffe yet and youre dreggys,
> As well borne as ye full oft tyme beggys.'
>
> ll. 6–7.

> . . . . . .

> As proud a pohen as ye sprede,
> Of me and other ye may haue nede.
>
> ll. 13–14.

The second poem[2] is of much greater interest. The
comely 'coystrowne,' or rascal, against whom this
extraordinary tirade is directed, appears to be a low-born
musician, who, much to Skelton's disgust, has gained
great success in his profession:

> For lordes and ladyes lerne at his scole: . . . .

Unfortunately however, puffed up by success, the 'comely
coystrowne' now imagines himself to be a gentleman, and
Skelton feels it is his duty to point out the true value of
his pretensions. He accuses him of being 'a holy water
clarke,' (the lowest of ecclesiastical officers), and abuses
his music:

> He lumbryth on a lewde lewte, Roty bully joyse,
> Rumbyll downe, tumbyll downe, hey go, now, now!
> He fumblyth in hys fyngeryng an vgly good noyse,
> It semyth the sobbyng of an old sow: . . . :
>
> ll. 29–32.

[1] Dyce, I, pp. 20–1. For a short consideration of the Mistress Anne poems see
L. J. Lloyd, *The Review of English Studies*, July, 1929.
[2] Dyce, I, pp. 15–17.

JOHN SKELTON

Finally he warns him not to carry his offensiveness too far:

> Ye are to vnhappy occasyons to fynde
> Vppon me to clater, or els to say yll.
>
> ll. 65–6.

The best is behind, and it behoves him to be careful.

Who the musician was is not known: the allusions are for the most part unintelligible. The interest of the poem lies in the fact that it is the earliest known example of Skelton's normal satirical procedure. This, briefly, consists of the piling up of unpleasant epithets upon the head of his opponent without the least regard either for decency or justice. The epithets are seemingly chosen more or less at random, but they are all distinguished by their offensiveness, and Skelton distributes them with an exceedingly lavish hand, packing his line almost to bursting point. Such a performance as *Agaynste a comely coystrowne* would be dull, or worse, if it were not for the gusto with which it is done. Skelton whoops and halloos with great glee, and his inventiveness and reckless handling of words gives a feeling of exhilaration to the verses. The poem gathers weight like a snowball: there seems to be no adequate reason why it should ever stop. When it does at last come to an end the reader is compelled to feel that Skelton only gives up because he is out of breath.

Incidentally it is worth pointing out that Skelton exhibits in this poem a wide acquaintance with musical terms, invariably used correctly.[1] It is not hard to picture him singing to the lute, the instrument upon which the 'comely coystrowne' so disgraced himself.

---

[1] See E. W. Naylor, *Music and the Poets*, 1927, for an excellent account of Skelton's knowledge of music. He would of course have studied music at Cambridge as an ordinary matter of academic routine; probably at least one book of the 'Music' of Boethius. It is worth noting that here for the first time Skelton introduces scraps of Latin into his verse. In this poem the quotations, 'Sospitati dedit aegros,' etc., are from the Missal, as the Rev. Dr. Adrian Morey kindly informed me.

Three further poems are worth a moment's notice; *Lullay, lullay lyke a chylde*, and *Manerly Margery*,[1] which are songs with refrains, and *Vppon a deedman's hed*.

Lullay, lullay has for its theme the reward meted out to a laggard lover, who loses his mistress while he is brutishly 'rowting' in his bed. She crosses the water, and finds another and more appreciative paramour:

> That halsyd her hartely and kyst her swete . . . .

and the poem ends with the crudely expressed opinion of the narrator:

> I wys, powle hachet, she bleryd thyne I.

Manerly Margery is an even rougher story of seduction, arranged in the form of a dialogue between a girl and the ubiquitous 'clerk'. Both these poems are full of vigour, and from a purely musical point of view *Manerly Margery* is perhaps the better of the two. They are undoubtedly well fitted to be sung: *Manerly Margery* was indeed set to music by William Cornishe, of the Chapel Royal,[2] whose setting still exists, though the music to *Lullay, lullay* has disappeared. Varied and telling epithets abound, as one would expect; the language has both pith and point:

> What dremyst thou, drunchard, drousy pate!
>   Thy lust and lykyng is from thé gone;
> Thou blynkerd blowboll, thou wakyst to late,
>   Behold, thou lyeste, luggard, alone!
>
> ll. 23–6.

The metre in both poems is identical, though the rhythm of *Manerly Margery* makes the poem march to better advantage; they are very fair specimens of their type.

Vppon a deedman's hed[3] is the earliest example of a poem written in the metre which Skelton was to make famous and which still bears his name. The theme of the poem is adequately displayed in Skelton's own preface:

[1] Dyce, I, pp. 22–3; pp. 28–9.
[2] Berdan, *op. cit.*, pp. 164–5.
[3] Dyce, I, pp. 18–20.

D   33

JOHN SKELTON

Vppon a deedmans hed, that was sent to hym from an honorable jentyllwoman for a token, deuysyd this gostly medytacyon in Englysh, couenable in sentence, comendable, lamentable, lacrymable, profytable for the soule.

The similarity between these verses and the elegy on Edward IV will be noticed at once. There is the same insistence upon the imminence of death and the impossibility of escape:

> For all oure pamperde paunchys,
> Ther may no fraunchys,
> Nor worldly blys,
> Redeme vs from this:
> Oure days be datyd,
> To be chekmatyd
> With drawttys of deth.

ll. 25–31.

The poem ends with a similar prayer:

> O goodly chyld
> Of Mary mylde,
> Then be oure shylde!
> That we be not exyld
> To the dyne dale
> Of boteles bale,
> Nor to the lake
> Of fendys blake.

ll. 41–48.

There is something faintly amusing in this solemn moralizing over poor Yorick, but it must be admitted that the dry, staccato, laconic phrases provide a perfect corollary to the grim nature of the theme. Skelton was to do infinitely greater things with his metre, but he never wrote anything more characteristic.

It has already been suggested that there is little in these early poems to rouse the lover of poetry to enthusiasm. There is indeed little in the whole of English poetry in the fifteenth century to interest anyone but the scholar. It can never cease to be surprising that, in England at

34

least, the great example of Chaucer was so poorly and ineptly followed. Lydgate, Hoccleve, Hawes and the rest are dead beyond any possibility of resurrection: Chaucer had pointed the way, but they had not the capacity to travel on it. It remained for Skelton alone to profit by his master's example, and, after trying his hand at many things, to strike out a path of his own.

These early poems therefore are interesting to the modern reader merely in so far as they contain indications of Skelton's qualities as a poet, and it happens that the information, albeit scanty and partial, is quite convincing, for Skelton's own peculiar brand of satire, courtly verse, ribaldry and verbal ingenuity is plainly foreshadowed.

It is clear beyond the possibility of doubt that when he sat down in his rectory at Diss to write *The Bowge of Courte* he was practised and skilful in the handling of English verse beyond any writer of his day. Moreover, nearly all his worldly triumphs were over, and the most fruitful part of his life was before him. His subsequent career can hardly have failed to surprise even such a man as he was. It certainly surprised his contemporaries, and continues to surprise us now, when his name is more familiar to the reader of poetry than it has been for four hundred years.

CHAPTER IV

THE BEGINNING OF A NEW CAREER

AS has been suggested earlier, it has been found impossible up to the present to discover exactly when Skelton removed, or was removed, to Diss, though it is tolerably certain that he was there in 1504. About 1504 therefore must be the date assigned to his first poem of any considerable length, *The Bowge of Courte*,[1] or *Court Rations*.

It is difficult to believe that the poem was written while its author was still a royal tutor, for it is an obvious if not particularized satire on the Court, with himself as the chief protagonist, full of angry bitterness and disillusion. It would be dangerous to theorize too freely, but from the internal evidence afforded by the poem it would appear that Skelton's career had collapsed into utter ruin through the machinations of numerous enemies, and that *The Bowge of Courte* is his carefully considered though impassioned comment on a piece of flagrant injustice. It is more than likely therefore that it was his first literary venture after he had retired from the environment which had finally proved so inimical to him, when the memory of his humiliation was still fresh in his mind.

Complaints about the miseries of the courtier's life are as old as courts, but there can hardly be in existence a more thorough-going condemnation than Skelton's picture of conditions in the court of Henry VII. His view, simply and plainly expressed, is that the Court is little but a happy-hunting ground for rascals, jealous of each other and continually racked by suspicion, fawning at once on a new arrival and ready to cast him off without ceremony

---

[1] Dyce, I, pp. 30–50. For earlier uses of the device of a ship see Koelbing: *Zur characteristik John Skeltons*, Stuttgart, 1904, pp. 69–82, and C. H. Herford: *The Literary Relations of England and Germany in the Sixteenth Century*, 1886, for much information relative to the poem.

if he falls into disfavour or becomes too dangerous. The prize they all seek so eagerly is merely an illusion. Fortune, to whom they trust their hopes, is the most fickle of mistresses.

At the lower end of the board are thieves, drunkards, and worse, who fritter their time away in debauchery, and find their chief diversion in the corruption of others less experienced in vice than themselves.

True merit cannot but go unrewarded in such a society as this; recognition can be obtained only by exercise of the most shameless sycophancy. A man of modest demeanour and genuine worth cannot exist in such an atmosphere; he must escape or perish.

These conclusions Skelton inevitably puts into allegorical dress when he comes to write down the history of his troubles. The academic and lover of traditional form in him naturally makes use of the dominant literary genre of the fifteenth century, and, more important still, allegory can be used to cover up what may not be brought out into the full light of day. It would be fruitless at this distance to attempt to identify the characters of the poem, save that we know that Drede, the hero, is Skelton himself, but this difficulty did not exist for his contemporaries. The drift of the criticism must have been recognized by many only too clearly.

Skelton seems to have feared this himself, for he appears anxious to dissociate himself from the opinions expressed by his characters. He reminds his readers that after all the story is only a dream: everyone is at liberty to interpret dreams in his own way:

> I wolde therwith no man were myscontente;
>   Besechynge you that shall it see or rede,
> In euery poynte to be indyfferente,
>   Syth all in substaunce of slumbrynge doth procede:
>   I wyll not saye it is mater in dede,
> But yet oftyme suche dremes be founde trewe:
> Now constrewe ye what is the resydewe.   ll. 533–539.

37

The story opens as Drede is falling asleep outside an inn at 'Harwich Port.' He dreams that he sees a stately vessel, *The Bowge of Courte*, come sailing into the harbour,

> Her takelynge ryche and of hye apparayle,

laden with 'royall marchaundyse.' The owner is Dame Saunce-pere, and what she has to sell is 'Fauore,' an expensive commodity:

> . . . who wyll haue it must paye therfore dere.

Drede goes on board, but is checked by Dame Saunce-pere's gentlewoman Daunger, who asks him why he is so impertinent as 'to press so proudly up,' and leaves him standing 'as a mased man' until Desyre, another gentle-woman, approaches, and consoles him by the loan of a jewel, Bone Auenture, advising him to try his fortune with it in the ship, and to mark Fortune, who is the pilot, very closely. Here the prologue ends, and the rest of the poem is concerned with the voyage, during which Drede is approached by

> Full subtyll persones, in nombre foure and thre,

who represent, as their names imply, the undesirable ele-ment in the life of courts. They are Fauell, 'full of flat-tery,' Suspecte, Haruy Hafter, Dysdayne, Ryotte, Dyssy-muler, and Subtylte. These rascals attempt to gain the confidence of the poet by abusing each other, but at length Drede sees various 'lewde felowes' plotting to kill him, and as they creep forward, 'of mortell entente,' he starts to leap over the side of the ship and awakes, takes pen and ink, and writes 'thys lytell boke.'

The Bowge of Courte is a true allegory, a worthy scion of a long line. Nowhere does Skelton show more clearly his complete mastery of the traditional material. But the poem is much more than an example of academic perfec-tion. In the words of a recent critic: 'I suppose that no reader has forgotten the vividness of its characters or its nightmare crescendo from guilelessness to suspicion,

THE BEGINNING OF A NEW CAREER

from suspicion to acute nervousness, and thence to panic
and awakening. The experience of a young man during
those painful years in which he first discovers that he has
entered a profession whose motto is "Dog eat Dog" could
hardly be better described.'[1] It is precisely this vividness,
as will be seen, which distinguishes Skelton from his
contemporaries and gives him his secure place in the
history of English poetry, but it is rarely seen unaccom-
panied. Old and new, mediaevalism and some new un-
known spirit, struggle for mastery to the end of the poet's
life. A merely casual reading of *The Bowge of Courte* might
indeed convey the impression that the poem is nothing
more than a vigorous and skilful example of traditional
allegory. It begins, for instance, with the stereotyped
astrological introduction:

> In autumpne, whan the sonne *in Virgine*
>   By radyante hete enryped hath our corne;
> Whan Luna, full of mutabylyte,
>   As emperes the dyademe hath worne
> Of our pole artyke, smylynge halfe in scorne
> At our foly and our vnstedfastnesse;
> The tyme/whan Mars to werre hym dyde dres; . . .
>
> ll. 1–7.

Skelton then proceeds to call to mind the ancient poets
who

> . . . full craftely,
> Vnder as couerte termes as coude be,
> Can touche a trouth and cloke it subtylly
> Wyth fresshe vtteraunce full sentencyously:
>
> ll. 9–12.

and expresses a wish that he might follow in their foot-
steps. With becoming modesty, however, he remembers
his own incapacity:

> But Ignoraunce full soone dyde me dyscure,
> And shewed that in this arte I was not sure;
> For to illumyne, she sayde, I was to dulle,

---

[1] C. S. Lewis, *The Allegory of Love*, Oxford, 1936, p. 252.

39

JOHN SKELTON

Auysynge me my penne awaye to pulle,
And not to wryte; . . . .

ll. 18–22.

Tired out by these perturbations Skelton falls asleep, and, of course, begins to dream immediately.

It is easy then to discover in the poem all the earmarks of the mediaeval type.[1] But there is a great deal in it which is far from typical mediaeval practice: traditional formulae are re-stated with Skelton's own peculiar originality and vigour. Vagueness is exchanged for clarity, the shadowy for the concrete. The poet falls asleep, but not as before, in a fair field, or in his chamber, from which

> He may on these braunches here
> The smale briddes singen clere
> Hir blisful swete song pitous.

Skelton falls asleep in very different surroundings, in an alehouse in the busy port of Harwich,

> In myne hostes house, called Powers Keye.

The poet dreams, but not of beautiful shadows. His companions are

> full subtyll persones, in nombre foure and thre,

rascals all, and real not only with the reality of nightmare, but with the actuality of the world of living men.

In his characterization of these rogues Skelton indeed almost breaks through the bonds of allegory altogether, for although the names he gives them—Riot, Disdain, Suspect, and so on—are of the traditional type, the characters themselves are so strongly marked that they almost succeed in coming alive. It is as though blood were starting to flow through the veins of waxworks. Consider for instance the description of Riot:

> Wyth that came Ryotte, russhynge all at ones,
> A rusty gallande, to-ragged and to-rente;
> And on the borde he whyrled a payre of bones,

---

[1] See Cesare Foligno in *The Legacy of the Middle Ages*, Oxford, 1926, p. 191.

THE BEGINNING OF A NEW CAREER

Quater treye dews he clatered as he wente;
  Now haue at all, by saynte Thomas of Kente!
And euer he threwe and kyst I wote nere what:
His here was growen thorowe oute his hat.

Thenne I behelde how he dysgysed was:
  His hede was heuy for watchynge ouer nyghte,
His eyen blereed, his face shone lyke a glas;
  His gowne so shorte that it ne couer myghte
  His rumpe, he wente so all for somer lyghte;
His hose was garded wyth a lyste of grene,
Yet at the knee they were broken, I wene.

ll. 344–357.

Such a *tour de force* as this is from the pen of no mere imitator of the best that has been thought and said: it is original and characteristic, and it is clearly the work of one on whom at least a portion of Chaucer's mantle has fallen. Not the least interesting of the other portraits is Skelton's picture of himself, in the person of the hero, Drede, a scholarly young man, diffident though by no means averse from friendship, anxious to do well, but completely unaware of the real nature of the world in which he hopes to succeed.

The varied assaults which are made against this raw young student by the rogues on board the ship are described with great brilliance: the action takes place in an atmosphere of double-dealing and hypocrisy, and the exposure of backstairs politicians is merciless and complete. As we read we seem to see figures moving stealthily along unlighted corridors, hiding behind curtains, listening at keyholes. Almost every species of rascality is reviewed and condemned. Skelton makes it very clear that Drede needs every ounce of his courage and common sense if he is to keep his head.

For instance, Harvy Hafter, the thief, masquerading as a plain blunt man, flatters him on his learning:

Loo, what is to you a pleasure grete,
  To haue that connynge and wayes that ye haue!

JOHN SKELTON

By Goddis soule, I wonder how ye gete
  Soo greate pleasyre, or who to you it gaue:
  Syr, pardone me, I am an homely knaue,
To be with you thus perte and thus bolde;
But ye be welcome to our housholde.

ll. 260-266.

He takes Drede into his confidence, and in the guise of
philosopher and friend attempts to scare him away by
telling him that although he has been on the ship for a
very long time he can even now scarcely make a bare
living. Dissimulation approaches Drede in much the
same way, praising him for his scholarship:

I knowe your vertu and your lytterature
  By that lytel connynge that I haue:
Ye be malygned sore, I you ensure;
  But ye haue crafte your selfe alwaye to saue:
  It is grete scorne to se a mysproude knaue
With a clerke that connynge is to prate:
Lete theym go lowse theym, in the deuylles date!

ll. 449-455.

Furthermore he offers Drede his support, offering to
share with him certain exclusive information about the
others. Riot prefers a more open method of attack;
abuses Drede for his studious habits, and attempts to lure
him to the gaming table. Disdain utters plain threats,
accusing Drede of making derogatory statements which
had never even entered his mind. He may as well realize
at once, he says, that he is causing annoyance to his
betters, who will 'shake him out of his clothes' if he does
not go home and leave the field to them. Deceit provides
a perfect example of that innuendo which more than
anything else characterizes for Skelton the life of courts:

But, by that Lorde that is one, two, and thre,
  I haue an errande to rounde in your ere:
He tolde me so, by God, ye maye truste me,
  Parde remembre whan ye were there,
  There I wynked on you,—wote ye not where?

42

THE BEGINNING OF A NEW CAREER

In A *loco*, I mene *juxta* B:
Woo is hym that is blynde and maye not see!

ll. 512–518.

One can almost see Deceit looking warily from side to side, winking, putting his finger against the side of his nose.

It is very much to Drede's credit that he keeps his balance in spite of this barrage of insinuation and threats, this varied display of chicanery. He stands his ground, but courage is not enough. The fight is seven to one, for the rogues combine in a common purpose to meet a common danger. Drede escapes from his dream-world only just in time: daggers are out.

The Bowge of Courte remains one of the best of Skelton's poems, possibly because it is one of the shortest. In this work his exuberant fancy is kept within proper limits by the exigencies of his chosen form, and he does not go on a moment too long. The language is terse, at times almost epigrammatic, full of force and colour. Characters and events are described with a vividness and sureness of touch which he was hardly ever to improve upon.

Harvy Hafter, Riot, and the rest of the rogues are the best sketches in this kind since Chaucer's pilgrims set out for Canterbury, and though there is a great gulf fixed between them and their earlier counterparts which Skelton was never great enough to bridge, they have still an air of authenticity about them, and they are worthy heralds of the living and breathing world of the Elizabethan stage.

Skelton has succeeded in this poem in pouring his new wine into the old bottles and in losing remarkably little of it in the process. It would be misleading to suggest that the bottles do not exist—*The Bowge of Courte* is thoroughly mediaeval and academic—but it is clear that it is the work of a man with a mind, purpose and will all his own, who has impressed with his own surprising individuality the materials which lay nearest to his hand.

43

JOHN SKELTON

A critic watching the literary horizon at the beginning of the sixteenth century could have been forgiven for seeing in *The Bowge of Courte* a new hope for English poetry.

CHAPTER V

'PHYLLYP SPAROWE'

IN Skelton's time there was a nunnery, Carowe by name, in the suburbs of Norwich. This nunnery, as Miss Eileen Power remarks, 'was a favourite resort for girls of noble and of gentle birth, but . . . was also recruited from the daughters of prosperous Norwich citizens.'[1] One of these girls was called Jane Scrope, and she had a pet sparrow, called Philip. But Gib the cat got it, and in so doing provided Skelton with the subject of what is perhaps his most delightful poem.

It is very unfortunate that nothing is known of his connection with Carowe, for this is the happiest time of his life. It is pleasant to picture him riding along, enjoying the countryside and his own peace of mind, being welcomed at Carowe as the famous scholar he is, listening afterwards to Jane's tearful recital of her misfortune. He has just written a satire. He has said his say. The Court is out of his system. Now he will write to please himself; write for the sheer joy of writing. And so Jane loses her pet, and so he writes another poem. But that is all we know of these first years at Diss, and it is much too little.

Phyllyp Sparowe[2] is a long poem—there are 1,400 lines of it—and it is an amazing mixture of poetry, comments on language and literature, burlesque, abuse and learning. Jane is of course the heroine, and when she is allowed to speak for herself the reader at once falls a willing captive to her freshness and charm. But Skelton will keep breaking in, throwing odds and ends of scholarship about, compiling catalogues, and using Jane as a kind of peg on which to hang a great deal of extraneous comment. Some

[1] *Mediaeval English Nunneries*, 1922, p. 12. See also Walter Rye, *Carrow Abbey*, 1889.
[2] Dyce, I, pp. 51-94.

of this comment is well worth hearing, particularly when it is concerned with Chaucer and the English language, but there is too much of it, and Skelton's fatal prolixity too often has its evil way with him.

There is no need to deprive him of the credit for his theme, though inevitable comparisons have been made with Catullus, Statius and Ovid. Even Catullus however can do little better than Skelton at his best:

> It was so prety a fole,
> It wold syt on a stole,
> And lerned after my scole
> For to kepe his cut,
> With, Phyllyp, kepe your cut!
> It had a veluet cap,
> And wold syt vpon my lap,
> And seke after small wormes,
> And somtyme white bred crommes;
> And many tymes and ofte
> Betwene my brestes softe
> It wolde lye and rest;
> It was propre and prest. ll. 115–127.

Poets writing on the same theme are likely somewhere to say much the same things: these things Skelton has in company with others, but here at any rate he is no plagiarist. The poem is a rambling affair, but there is some attempt at a plan, for it can be divided into three parts; a lament for the sparrow, ostensibly by Jane; a eulogy of Jane by the poet; and finally, his protest against unfair criticism. Further subdivided these parts form ten more, unequal in length, but there is no organic relation between the parts, and they may perhaps reveal the way in which the poem was composed, in joyous and carefree fashion, in brief bursts of enthusiasm.

Jane's lament, with which the poem opens, is beautifully done, in Skelton's most engaging and delicate manner, and it contains some of the most charming lines in the work:

46

Somtyme he wolde gaspe
Whan he sawe a waspe;
A fly or a gnat,
He wolde flye at that;
And prytely he wold pant
Whan he saw an ant;
Lord, how he wolde pry
After the butterfly!
Lorde, how he wolde hop
After the gressop!
And whan I sayd, Phyp, Phyp,
Than he wold lepe and skyp,
And take me by the lyp.
Alas, it wyll me slo,
That Phillyp is gone me fro!

ll. 128–142.

And again:

I toke my sampler ones,
Of purpose, for the nones,
To sowe with stytchis of sylke
My sparow whyte as mylke,
That by representacyon
Of his image and facyon,
To me it myght importe
Some pleasure and comforte
For my solas and sporte:
But whan I was sowing his beke,
Methought, my sparow did speke,
And opened his prety byll,
Saynge, Mayd, ye are in wyll
Agayne me for to kyll,
Ye prycke me in the head!
With that my nedle waxed red,
Methought, of Phyllyps blode;
Myne hear ryght vpstode,
And was in suche a fray,
My speche was taken away.   ll. 210–229.

Gib, as might be expected, comes in for a great deal of abuse; fifty lines of it, packed with unpleasantness which

Jane wishes may be visited upon the whole feline race.
Even after the main storm has spent itself there is an
occasional rumble of thunder:

> And it were a Jewe,
> It wolde make one rew,
> To se my sorow new.
> These vylanous false cattes
> Were made for myse and rattes,
> And not for byrdes smale.
> Alas, my face waxeth pale
> Tellynge this pyteyus tale . . .

ll. 335–342.

> Whan I remembre it,
> How pretely it wolde syt,
> Many tymes and ofte,
> Vpon my fynger aloft!
> I played with him tyttell tattyll,
> And fed him with my spattyl,
> With his byll betwene my lippes;
> It was my prety Phyppes!
> Many a prety kusse
> Had I of his swete musse;
> And now the cause is thus,
> That he is slayne me fro,
> To my great payne and wo.

ll. 353–365.

After this pathetic exordium Jane calls on all manner
of birds to come and weep with her at the funeral, and
there is an immediate and gratifying response to her
request; for, as if they had heard of Skelton's fondness for
long lists, no fewer than seventy-seven birds appear and
are presented with their appropriate offices in a burlesque
of the Roman Burial Service. Most of the birds are
merely mentioned by name, but Skelton pauses over a
few of particular interest and describes them in succinct
and amusing little sketches:

> The storke also,
> That maketh his nest

In chymneyes to rest;
Within those walles
No broken galles
May there abyde
Of cokoldry syde,
Or els phylosophy
Maketh a great lye.   ll. 469–477.

    The estryge, that wyll eate
An horshowe so great,
In the stede of meate,
Such feruent heat
His stomake doth freat;
He can not well fly,
Nor synge tunably,
Yet at a brayde
He hath well assayde
To solfe aboue ela,
Ga, lorell, fa, fa; . . . .
                                            ll. 478–488.

Perhaps the most successful of these portraits is that of
the Phoenix:

    The byrde of Araby,
That potencyally
May neuer dye,
And yet there is none
But one alone;
A phenex it is
This herse that must blys
With armatycke gummes
That cost great summes,
The way of thurifycation
To make a fumigation,
Swete of reflary,
And redolent of eyre,
This corse for to sence
With greate reuerence,
As patryarke or pope
In a blacke cope; . . . .   ll. 513–529.

All the birds do their duty, and at last Phyllyp is buried, with a long Latin epitaph over his grave. '*Flos volucrum formose, vale!*' says Jane sadly, and leaves the rest of the poem to her sympathetic friend, who comes forward upon the stage in his own person to describe her for the benefit of his readers. The 'Commendacions,' as this part of the poem is called, is a surprise, for its tone is by no means that of a priest describing a young boarder at a nunnery. Jane has in fact turned into the typical mistress of a mediaeval poet, with 'eyen gray and stepe' like those of the Prioress, veins of 'Indy saphyre blew,' and 'lips emblomed lyke the chery.' Her hair, needless to say, is golden, and it shines like the beams of Phoebus. But she is a beauty with a difference: Skelton is the soul of truth, and he admits that

> Her beautye to augment,
> Dame Nature hath her lent
> A warte vpon her cheke.

ll. 1041–3.

But this is no blemish. Indeed, as he somewhat humour-lessly points out, it appears

> . . . from afar,
> Lyke to the radyant star,
> All with fauour fret,
> So properly it is set: . . . .

ll. 1046–9.

Hyperbole (or burlesque) can go no further, but the whole episode is characteristic of Skelton's independence. One cannot help suspecting that the wart is there for a purpose, and that Skelton himself is a little tired of the perfections of other poets' mistresses.

Nevertheless, he is full of admiration: so much so that he doubts his capacity to convey a just picture of his lady: his reason is 'rude and dul':

> How shall I report
> All the goodly sort
> Of her fetures clere,

50

That hath non erthly pere?
The fauour of her face
Ennewed all with grace,
Confort, pleasure, and solace,
Myne hert doth so enbrace,
And so hath rauyshed me
Her to behold and se,
That in wordes playne
I cannot me refrayne
To loke on her agayne:
. Alas, what shuld I fayne?
It wer a pleasaunt payne
With her aye to remayne.

ll. 998–1013.

New graces appear with her every movement:

But whereto shulde I note
How often dyd I tote
Vpon her prety fote?
It raysed myne hert rote
To se her treade the grounde
With heles short and rounde.
She is playnly expresse
Egeria, the goddesse,
And lyke to her image,
Emportured with corage,
A louers pylgrimage;....

ll. 1145–55.

She is second to none: Diana, Venus, Pallas, Lucretia, Polixena and Calliope are all compared with her and found wanting. She is 'the lode star of delyght, and the well of worldly treasure,' worthy

to be enrolde
With letters of golde.
Car elle vault.

So Skelton rushes on, enthusiasm and gusto leading him on to one extravagance after another. One may legitimately wonder what Jane thought of all this, if she ever saw it. There can be little doubt that she was the

51

Rector's inspiration, in spite of her traditional grey eyes and 'sydes long and streyte.' There is that wart, and a 'sker upon her chyn' to consider. The 'Commendacions' is divided into eleven parts, ten of which end with a refrain:

> For this most goodly floure,
> This blossome of fresshe couloure,
> So Jupiter me soccour,
> She floryssheth new and new
> In beaute and vertew:
> *Hac claritate gemina*
> *O gloriosa foemina,*

which is completed by a Latin couplet, changed each time. This, for example, is the first refrain in its complete form:

> For this most goodly floure,
> This blossome of fresshe coulour,
> So Jupiter me socour,
> She floryssheth new and new
> In bewte and vertew:
> *Hac claritate gemina*
> *O gloriosa foemina,*
> *Retribue servo tuo, vivifica me!*
> *Labia mea laudabunt te.*

ll. 893–901.

This light-hearted dealing with things serious and sacred cannot have commended itself to everyone, and it seems that critics arose and spoke their minds, though whether they objected to the Latin or to other things it is not easy to see. Their opinion however was clearly expressed, and in the 'Commendacions' Skelton pauses for a moment to comment on it. A certain Envy (possibly Alexander Barclay, no friend to Skelton)

> With his ledder ey,
> And chekes dry,

had declared that all this praise of Jane was nothing but wasted effort:

'PHYLLYP SPAROWE'

Sayth that I
Vse great folly
For to endyte,
And for to wryte,
And spend my tyme
In prose and ryme,
For to expres
The noblenes
Of my maistres.

ll. 950–8.

The 'Commendacions' finished, Skelton returns to the attack and hits out fiercely, declaring that his enemies are jealous of his success, calling on the spirit of Philip and swearing by a list of classical personages fifty lines long ranging from Hercules to Charon, who

. . . with his frownsid fore top
Gydeth his bote with a prop.

He cannot understand, he says, what there is to complain of: Philip will perhaps be able to tell him.

If this attitude is taken up so as to throw dust into the eyes of his opponents it is very poorly done. He knew very well what the trouble was. In the first place he had attempted something new: in itself that was an offence. Moreover, to the adherents of the allegorical school *Phyllyp Sparowe* must have appeared a piece of tasteless buffoonery, to the orthodox churchman a wilful travesty of much that was sacred and venerable. To begin a poem with a quotation from the Office for the Dead and invoke Jupiter ninety lines later was a form of amusement difficult for some to condone. One wishes that Caxton's opinion of *Phyllyp Sparowe* had survived, for many of Skelton's admirers must have felt that they had in some sort been betrayed into the hands of the enemy. To make matters worse, Skelton had incorporated classical references—even aureate terms—into a lilting doggerel with neither tradition nor reason behind it. And to confound confusion still further he had achieved an instantaneous

53

popularity with his new measure. To the Humanist, who cared nothing for the vernacular, the novelty of the new poetry made no appeal, and whatever sympathy Skelton's scholarship may have obtained for him vanished in disgust at this perpetuation of a mediaeval form of versification. It is indeed difficult to think of anything more remote from Cicero, the God of them all. But henceforward he was to write the greater part of his work in the despised metre, since it suited his peculiar purposes to perfection.

It was, as he used it, his own invention, though something very similar had appeared much earlier, and there can be little doubt as to its origin. These 'rhyming trimeter lines forming a verse paragraph closed by one dimeter line' come from the heart of the Middle Ages, from the wandering scholars, whose songs still blossom in the dust of a hundred forgotten controversies. Carried about from Paris to Padua, from Padua to Oxford and back again, telling of the pleasures of love, wine and the well-laden board, shaped by many hands but the property of none, these lyrics bring once again before our eyes the mediaeval student in his habit as he lived, walking the roads in rain and sun, stretching out his toes to a tavern fire; deciding, in an access of gratitude towards all taverns, to die at last in the sweet fumes of ale.[1]

The student poet had only himself and his friends to please, and his songs do not for the most part suggest conscious literary artifice. But constant passage from mouth to mouth resulted in a polish, conciseness and spontaneity which perhaps could hardly have been otherwise achieved. These songs remain to show what could still be done with Latin by those who used it not only because they must, but because they loved it.

Skelton must have known, and enjoyed, many of these songs at Cambridge; it is at least possible that he got his

[1] For a full account of these lyrics see the delightful monograph by Miss Helen Waddell, *The Wandering Scholars*, 1927, and especially chapter 12.

first inspiration from them. But there is another suggestion to be considered. He may have seen Ranulf Higden's
Polychronicon, and read in that work the following description of Wales:

> Libri finis nunc Cambriam
> Prius tangit quam Angliam;
> Sic propero ad Walliam.
> Ad Priami prosapiam;
> Ad magni Jovis sanguinem,
> Ad Dardani progeniem.
> Sub titulis his quatuor
> Terrae statum exordior;
> Primo de causa nominis;
> Secundo de praeconiis;
> Tandem de gentis ritibus;
> Quarto de mirabilibus.[1]

Again, he might also have seen Trevisa's translation of
Higden, written in 1387:

> Now þe book takeþ in honde
> Wales to fore Engelonde;
> So I take my tales
> And wende forþ in to Wales,
> To that noble brood
> Of Priamus his blood,
> Knoweleche for to wynne
> Of greet Iubiter his kynne,
> For to haue in mynde
> Dardanus his kynde.
> In þis foure titles I fonde
> To telle þe state of þat londe.
> Cause of þe name I schall telle,
> And þan preise þe lond I welle.
> Then I schal write wiþ my pen
> Alle þe maneres of þe men.
> Then I schal fonde
> To tell mervailes of þe londe.

---

[1] Berdan, *op. cit.*, pp. 168–70. I am also indebted to Professor Berdan for the examples which follow.

However this may be, he could hardly have avoided Caxton's revision of Trevisa, which he published, together with Higden's Latin, in 1482, changing as he thought necessary 'the rude and old Englysch, that is to wete certeyn wordes which in these dayes be neither vsyd ne understanden', so that the translation might conform to modern standards:

> Now this book taketh on honde
> Wales after Englond,
> So take I my tales,
> And wende into Wales,
> To that noble brood
> Of Priamus blood,
> Knoleche for to wynne
> Of grete Jupiters kynne,
> For to have in mynde
> Dardanus kynde.
> In thise foure titles I fonde
> To alle the state of that londe;
> Cause of the nam I shall telle;
> And then preyse the lond and welle;
> Then I shall write with my penne
> Alle the maners of the menne;
> Thenne I shall fonde
> To telle mervailles of the londe.

Now this is not 'Skeltonical' verse, but it is near enough to it to interest a man who perhaps is already more than half-way on the road towards something of the kind. In any case it is clear that Skelton had at least two kinds of tradition to draw upon. Incidentally it is worth noticing that Skeltonics in Latin were regarded by the Humanists as characteristic of the barbarous Middle Ages. Thus *Petrus Nigelinus*, in the *Epistolae Obscurorum Virorum*, is made to write:

> Sancte Petre domine
> nobis miserere,
> Quia tibi dominus
> dedit cum istis clavibus

56

'PHYLLYP SPAROWE'

Potestatem maximam,
necnon specialem gratiam
Super omnes sanctos:
quia tu es privilegiatus,
Quod solvis est solutum,
in terris et per caelum,
Et quicquid hic ligaveris,
ligatum est in caelis. . . .

and so on, in the manner of a negligible Latinist hope-
lessly out of date. But it was in a happy hour that Skelton
decided to try his hand at a long poem in his newly-
invented measure, for the success of *Phyllyp Sparowe* con-
vinced him beyond any doubt that he had found a
medium which suited what may perhaps be called his
secular purposes to perfection. He never deserted aureate
and polished terms, nor did he lose his very real affection
for them, but henceforth all that was most vital in his
work found expression in this odd and delightful metre.

In the first place he found it extremely adaptable. His
was a restless mind, constantly reaching out after new
ideas, allusions, words. No sooner does he settle down
than he is up again: no sooner does he begin to play
with a new notion than he discards it. Much of *Phyllyp
Sparowe* reminds one of a coloured ball being tossed
rapidly from hand to hand. But the verse can easily carry
such thought as there is, and the short nervous line and
felicitous rhyming convey to the reader a feeling of
exhilaration which had been a stranger to English literature for many years. *Phyllyp Sparowe* is too long, too
incoherent and too facile; but it is alive, too alive perhaps
to please many of Skelton's contemporaries. Their opinions, however, had no sort of effect. Skelton's reply was
to leave a curse with them, and to proceed at once to
another poem in the same style.

Luride, cur, livor, volucris pia funera damnas?
Talia te rapiant rapiunt quae fata volucrem!
Est tamen invidia mors tibi continua.

Such is his unrepentant conclusion. And so ends what might so easily have been one of the most significant poems in the language, though Skelton himself makes no claim to innovation. As it happened however development was to lie in a totally different direction, and so rapid was it to be that within sixty years after his death he was dismissed ignominiously, as a 'rude railing rhymster,' by Thomas Puttenham, busying himself about the art of poetry in 1584. The Renaissance was to force early English poetry temporarily into the background, and it soon became necessary to apologize even for Chaucer, though he never lost his fascination for those of true poetic temper. For the rest, it was the product of an age of barbarism, and deserved to be treated with nothing but pity and contempt. Skelton naturally shared the fate of his fellows, and it was a long time before any sympathetic inquiries were made into his merits.

For it must not be supposed that Skelton was the only writer to follow mediaeval precedent in the matter of metre and verse construction. Nothing it is true has survived in bulk from any one author; many poems are anonymous, and obviously only a fragment of the output remains. There is however nothing of the calibre of *Phyllyp Sparowe* among these survivals, though much is noteworthy. Furthermore there is nothing in Skeltonical verse which even approaches his own peculiar success.

After *Phyllyp Sparowe* Skelton does little but ring the changes on his former work. There is hardly anything among his later writings, apart from *Magnyfycence*, which differs essentially in construction from *The Bowge of Courte* or *Phyllyp Sparowe*, and even his isolated return to allegory in *The Garlande of Laurell* lies somewhat outside the main line of development. In the metre of *Phyllyp Sparowe* he had found what he considered to be his ideal medium. The ease with which he could handle it delighted his excitable and vivacious mind. The terseness of the short five-syllable line lent itself at once to vigorous thrusts and the employment of violent abuse, and as we have seen he could easily turn it on occasion into a tripping measure of extreme delicacy and charm.

With its inherent dangers he seems to have had little concern, though he probably recognized them clearly enough. His next poem, *Elynour Rummynge*, ends with a remark which may not unfairly be construed as a realization of the fatal facility of his verse. He pulls himself up short for no apparent reason with the words:

> I haue wrytten to mytche
> Of this mad mummynge
> Of Elynour Rummynge.
> Thus endeth the gest
> Of this worthy fest.

No doubt other considerations combined to cause this exclamation, but in any case it is a conclusion which might apply equally well to almost anything to which he later set his hand. He never returned, save once, to the sheer pleasant exuberance of *Phyllyp Sparowe*, though there is vigour enough of another sort in his next poem. Henceforward he was to employ his pen on greater matters than the death of a sparrow, which, as Mr. Pepys might have said, is a pity.

CHAPTER VI

WORDS, WORDS, WORDS

I

'ELYNOUR RUMMYNGE'

*T*HE *Tunnyng of Elynour Rummynge*[1] must have silenced some of Skelton's critics for ever. *Phyllyp Sparowe* had been a mistake, and they had dutifully pointed this out; but this new production was unspeakable, completely beneath the notice of scholars. To criticize such things, even to read them, was something not to be thought of for a moment. To reply to just strictures by writing a long string of low verses on an equally low theme was to place oneself beyond the pale. Evidently the man was now lost to all sense of propriety. As so often happens, however, the critic's loss is the reader's gain. This riotous description of an ale-wife and her clientèle, formless and completely unsubtle as it is, is the most vigorous poem Skelton ever wrote; an imperishable testimony to the strength and essential sanity of his mind; a delightful exhibition of honest animal spirits. There had been nothing like it since the *Canterbury Tales*.

Elynour Rummynge lived at Leatherhead, but what Skelton was doing there does not appear. It may be that she represents an ale-wife a little nearer home. At any rate Skelton represents himself sitting in a corner of her tavern, watching the women coming in to sample the new brew, and bringing with them all manner of gifts to pay for their drinks. He sits and watches: nothing escapes him. Every woman is described in turn with merciless accuracy: no detail is too gross to be noted down. The authenticity of the poem is clearly beyond question. A

[1] Dyce, I, pp. 95-115.

60

kind of prologue is devoted to Elynour herself, who is
described with a wealth of pungent detail which prepares
the reader for what is to come. Then the customers are
reviewed in turn, and it appears that each newcomer is, if
possible, more unprepossessing than the last: of all might
it be said, as Skelton says of Elynour,

> . . . her vysage
> It would aswage
> A mannes courage. . . .

the courage, that is, of any man but Skelton, whose
stomach can stand anything.

Of all these portraits only that of Elynour is near to
success, perhaps because she is shown with a greater
wealth of detail, paused over as it were and realized,
whereas most of the others are dealt with at too great a
pace, and are not so much characters as strings of epithets.
The single details are plausible enough, but they are so
embroidered and overweighted that they tend to lose a
great deal of their effect. Within the walls of the tavern,
however, the company does not seem in the least incongruous: the reader is hypnotized by Skelton's exuberance,
and while the spell lasts he is prepared to endure a willing
suspension of disbelief until the last couplet has spent
itself like an expiring rocket.

Certainly Elynour is conceived more or less in the
round: she may indeed be drawn from life. But such a
mass of unpleasant detail is thrust upon the reader that
even her outlines tend to become shadowy or distorted.
We hear of her 'lothely lere,' her 'lewde lyppes,' and her
'skynne lose and slacke.' Her nose is 'somdele hoked,' and
she is 'jawed lyke a jetty.' But in spite of all this she is by
no means without self-confidence, and more than a
touch of vanity:

> She thynketh herselfe gaye
> Vpon the holy daye,
> Whan she doth her aray,

And gyrdeth in her gytes
Stytched and pranked with pletes;
Her kyrtel Brystow red,
With clothes vpon her hed
That wey a sowe of led,
Wrythen in wonder wyse,
After the Sarasyns gyse,
With a whym wham,
Knyt with a trym tram,
Vpon her brayne pan,
Lyke an Egyptian,
Capped about:
Whan she goeth out
Herselfe for to shewe,
She dryueth downe the dewe
Wyth a payre of heles
As brode as two wheles;
She hobles as a gose
With her blanket hose
Ouer the falowe;
Her shone smered wyth talowe,
Gresed vpon dyrt
That baudeth her skyrt.

ll. 65–90.

One cannot help thinking of the Wife of Bath very much the worse for wear.[1] But Elynour feels herself to be still attractive and desirable: it is the result, she says, of drinking her own ale:

Beholde, she sayde, and se
How bryght I am of ble!
Ich am not cast away,
That can my husband say,
Whan we kys and play

[1] Her coverchiefs full fyne were of ground;
I dorste swere they weyeden ten pound
That on a Sonday were upon her heed.
Her hosen weren of fyn scarlet reed,
Full streite y-teyd, and shoos ful moiste and newe.
Bold was her face, and fair, and reed of hewe.
Prologue to *The Canterbury Tales*, ll. 453–8.

WORDS, WORDS, WORDS

In lust and in lykyng;
He calleth me his whytyng,
His mullyng and his mytyng,
His nobbes and his conny,
His swetyng and his honny,
With Bas, my pretty bonny
Thou art worth good and monny,
This make I my falyre fonny,
Til that he dreme and dronny;
For, after all our sport,
Than wyll he rout and snort;
Than swetely together we ly,
As two pygges in a sty.

ll. 217–34.

Her gossips are a fearsome crew; not only for the most part ill-favoured, but coarse, dirty, greedy and vindictive. But Skelton thoroughly enjoys himself: like Chaucer, he rejoices in everything that is good 'in its kind'; and these are superb sluts:

Than Margery Mylkeducke
Her kyrtell she did vptucke
An ynche aboue her kne,
Her legges that ye myght se;
But they were sturdy and stubbed,
Myghty pestels and clubbed,
As fayre and as whyte
As the fote of a kyte:
She was somwhat foule,
Crokenecked lyke an oule;
And yet she brought her fees,
A cantell of Essex chese,
Was well a fote thycke,
Full of maggottes quycke;
It was huge and greate,
And myghty stronge meate
For the deuyll to eate;
It was tart and punyete.   ll. 418–435.

Skelton indeed approves of them so much that at one

63

point he joins the 'foule drabbes' to jeer at the only customer who seems to have something of respectability about her:

> But, syr, among all
> That sat in that hall,
> There was a pryckemedenty,
> Sat lyke a seynty,
> And began to paynty,
> As thoughe she would faynty;
> She made it as koy
> As a lege de moy;
> She was not halfe so wyse
> As she was peuysshe nyse.
> She sayde neuer a worde,
> But rose from the borde,
> And called for our dame,
> Elynour by name. ll. 580–593.

One thing at any rate is certain. Such observation as this does not come from the study. Skelton's acquaintance with taverns, like that of many great men before and after him, was more than academic. But he never loses complete control either of himself or his poem, and towards the end he turns aside to laugh at his own extravagance:

> Now truly, to my thynkynge,
> This is a solempne drinkynge.

Very soon afterwards he winds up the party, for no apparent reason except that he thinks he has done enough, or more than enough perhaps:

> I haue wrytten to mytche
> Of this mad mummynge
> Of Elynour Rummynge.

'To mytche' or no, he had produced a unique piece of work, and given himself full scope for the expression of his delight in various manifestations of the physical and the concrete. And once again he had indulged to the full his passion for rich and strange words, which, if not

64

Wedges of gold, great anchors, heaps of pearl,
Inestimable stones, unvalued jewels,

are yet vigorous and pithy, expressive, powerful and honest.

It cannot be denied, however, that with all its great merits *Elynour Rummynge* is probably the poem which above all others has contributed to blacken Skelton's reputation in the eyes of posterity. Pope's 'beastly Skelton' no doubt has his origin here, and many subsequent critics have done little but echo this jibe. *Elynour Rummynge* is indeed full of expressions which, like Margery Mylkeducke's cheese, are 'tart and punyete', frankly crude, the catchwords of those whose habitation is in the lowest haunts. But ordinary Tudor coarseness could easily be pleaded in extenuation, if an apology were needed. The plain fact is however that the good humour and gusto of the poem are easily able to carry any sort of language: it will be a strange reader who is seriously perturbed by this sort of horseplay. Skelton is often coarse, but he is seldom, if ever, offensive, and his complete honesty and frank approach to his subject are completely disarming. There is nothing offensive about a farmyard, and it cannot be too strongly urged, not only for Skelton but also for his epoch, that Tudor language, however offensive sometimes to modern ears, at least contains few traces of that far more insidious suggestiveness, that polished and refined literary eroticism which the following century was to borrow from Italy and which reaches its apotheosis in Sterne. No one in his senses would suggest that *Elynour Rummynge* has anything to do with refinement, but it is at least a great deal more wholesome than much of *A Sentimental Journey*.

II

'AGAINST GARNESCHE'

Words, in their inexhaustible variety, are also the main interest of a group of poems written against Sir Christopher Garnesche as part of a 'flyting' or literary combat between him and Skelton.

Sir Christopher's name appears more than once in contemporary records,[1] but of the causes of his quarrel with Skelton nothing whatever is known, though Skelton himself states his own side of the question fairly clearly. There are four of these poems, or diatribes,[2] and they vary both in length and in metre. The most interesting thing about them is that they end with the words 'Be the kynges most noble commandement'; and this phrase has given a certain amount of colour to the supposition that Skelton was indeed a poet laureate in the modern sense of the term. Even if Skelton wrote the words himself they are far from proving the fact that his poetical office was of a permanent kind, though the idea that Henry VIII, at this time a comparatively young man notoriously full of boisterous energy, should have staged a poetical combat between a well-known scholar and a gentleman-usher is far from being improbable. Henry at any rate would probably have derived considerable amusement from this interchange of mud-slinging.

Skelton states emphatically that Garnesche was responsible for the beginning of the quarrel, but his remarks are somewhat obscure:

> Sithe ye haue me chalyngyd, M(aster) Garnesche,
> Ruduly revilyng me in the kynges noble hall,
> Soche an odyr chalyngyr cowde me no man wysch,
> But yf yt war Syr Termagant that tyrnyd with out nall;
> For Syr Frollo de Franko was neuer halfe so talle.
> But sey me now, Syr Satrapas, what autoryte ye haue
> In your chalenge, Syr Chystyn, to cale me knaue?[3]
>
> ll. 1-7.

From other insinuations scattered about the poems it

---

[1] Dyce, I, xxx–xxxiv.

[2] Dyce, I, pp. 116–131. These 'flytings' were a common form of literary amusement: the most famous was between Dunbar and Walter Kennedy. See George Saintsbury: *Short History of English Literature*, 1922, pp. 187–8, and S. M. Tucker: *Verse Satire in England before the Renaissance*, 1908.

[3] Dyce, I, p. 116.

appears that Garnesche had called Skelton a knave and a
'lorell'; had disparaged his ancestry, and described him
as 'scalled and mad'; had cast scorn upon his laurel
crown, and suggested that he ought to be hanged.
These are only a few specimens from the list. In return
for these remarks, Skelton provides the most astonishing
amount of sheer abuse that can ever have come from the
pen of a literary antagonist. The range of his epithets is,
to say the least, bewildering; but when the smoke of
battle has blown away, it is possible to see that these
poems are merely the performance for which *Agaynste a
comely coystrowne* was in some sort a rehearsal.

It will be noticed at once that although the poems
Against Garnesche are full of much more elaborate matter,
the method of procedure is precisely the same. Skelton
attempts to convince his readers that Garnesche is a man
of humble origin who has risen to his present eminence
from the most menial of situations:

> Whan ye war yonger of age,
> Ye war a kechyn page,
> A dyshwasher, a dryvyll,
> In the pott your nose dedde sneuyll;
> Ye fryed and ye broylyd,
> Ye rostyd and ye boylyd,
> Ye rostyd, lyke a fonne,
> A gose with the fete vponne;
> Ye slvfferd vp sowse
> In my lady Brewsys howse.
> Wherto xulde I wryght
> Of soche a gresy knyght?
> A bawdy dyscheclowte,
> That bryngeth the world abowte
> With laftinge and with polleynge,
> With lyenge and controlleynge.[1]

ll. 24–39.

The same tactics are used against Wolsey later:
Skelton seems to have imagined that this particular type

[1] Dyce, I, p. 120.

of reviling was one of the strongest and most effective
weapons in his armoury.

A great deal is made of Garnesche's knighthood, which
seems to rankle in Skelton's mind:

> Thow claimist thé jentyll, thou art a curre;
> Haroldis they know thy cote armur:

and he compares his enemy satirically with many re-
nowned paladins, and with others whose reputations
have completely vanished:

> Syr Gy, Syr Gawen, Syr Cayus, for and Syr Olyuere,
> Pyramus, nor Priamus, nor syr Pyrrus the prowde,
> In Arturys auncyent actys no where ys prouyd your pere;
> The facyoun of your fysnamy the devyl in a clowde;
> Your harte is to hawte, I wys, yt wyll nat be alowde.
> Ye capyd Cayfas copyus, your paltoke on your pate,
> Thow ye prate lyke prowde Pylate, be ware of cheke mate.[1]

ll. 22–28.

As usual, Skelton scatters names and references indis-
criminately: it is more than likely that half the knights he
mentions in this poem never existed outside his own
fertile imagination. He returns again and again to this
attack throughout the series, and together with sneers at
Garnesche's low birth and lack of skill in letters it forms
the main staple of the coherent part of his satire.

It is surprising to see Skelton admitting at one point
that Garnesche is a good musician: 'thowthe ye kan
skylle of large and longe,' he says. But this is the only
example of generosity to be found in all this scurrility.
Most of it is indeed nothing but personal abuse of a
particularly virulent type. Garnesche's appearance, habits,
love-affairs, manners, and abilities are brought into merciless review, and adorned with a singular collection of
epithets and incomprehensible allusions, which serve
only to befog and irritate the reader. Humour is not
entirely absent, but it is in any case very different from the
boisterous and open-hearted fooling of *Elynour Rum-*

[1] Dyce, I, p. 119.

mynge. Mere railing, obviously bearing no relation whatever to the true state of affairs, is offensive even in the hands of genius—few read the poems of even Swift—and as far as these poems are concerned Skelton has very little genius in his composition. Dyce thought that 'a real animosity seems to have existed between our author and his adversary,' but it must be confessed that these verses bear little testimony to genuine feeling of any kind. The general impression is that of a man working himself up into a fury to order, and though there is more than enough unpleasantness in the performance there is no trace of real malignity. There are moreover numerous signs of strain and an unusual air of breathlessness and exhaustion in the poems, and they make tedious reading, though one may wonder once again at Skelton's virtuosity and resource in the elaboration of nauseous images.

One may hope that if ever Henry saw them he enjoyed the outcome of his most noble commandment, for posterity has not been interested.

Against Garnesche does at any rate provide an excellent and salutary contrast to the infinitely more valuable *Elynour Rummynge*. The danger is that they may both be conveniently left under the same label, considered equally as typical productions of the beastly Skelton. *Against Garnesche* is Skelton at his worst; the poems are practically worthless from every point of view, though even here vivid phrases occasionally strike the reader's attention: it would be strange if it were not so. Such things as 'Your wynde schakyn shankkes, 'As wytles as a wylde goos,' 'Cicero with hys tong of golde' show that the real Skelton is not quite asleep, but such felicities are rare.

The Skelton of the Wolsey poems is however now clearly foreshadowed, and it is easy to see from the sure touch of *Elynour Rummynge*, and the more doubtful resources of this command performance, what manner of man holds the Rectory of Diss. And it is possible to see in some measure what he will do when he is genuinely

69

moved in a cause far removed from his own personal feelings. He is already the most formidable satirist in England, since he is not interested in abstruse speculation, and is not concerned, save at rare moments, with political allegory. He states his case as plainly and forcefully as he can. Much was to happen before he was so roused, but his materials are ready, and all that is lacking is a fitting subject on which to use them.

III

'WARE THE HAUKE'

There can be no doubt that Skelton would have been profoundly shocked and extremely indignant had anyone, with *Elynour Rummynge* or *Against Garnesche* in mind, suggested that there was anything about him which was unbecoming in the rector of a parish. To-day, even if we are prepared to consider him as something more than a coarse and cantankerous Merry-Andrew, he appears to be a somewhat strange parson, though there can be no doubt that he was an honest priest. But he himself had no qualms, for he was not only a pious man and a faithful son of the Church: he was proud of his priesthood and jealous of the dignity of his office. As he looked about him he saw many priests who, as he thought, had no conception whatever of the sanctity of their position, who were lost to all sense of decorum, and no better than clods. His indignation against such as these may strike some modern readers as a little strange, but it did not seem so to him, for he was satisfied that he had nothing to reproach himself with—if he ever thought about the matter at all. And indeed one may look in vain in his work for any mockery of things sacred (there was nothing unusual about the burlesque in *Phyllyp Sparowe*), or any suggestion that he took his duties casually. On the contrary, what he regarded as irreverence he took very seriously indeed: he could hardly find words strong enough to express his disapproval of it. As it happened, a particularly gross piece of clerical boorishness was thrust before his notice in his own parish, in his own church. He was moved to express his anger in verse, and for a very good reason he called his poem *Ware the Hauke.*

One morning, he says, when he was passing his church, he heard an appalling din, coming without any doubt, from inside. He rushed to the door, and found it shut,

> Fast boltyd and barryd,

but he managed to get in through his private entrance, and there a sight met his eyes which it took him a few seconds to assimilate. The church was in hopeless confusion. Hawks were flying about, and one had perched itself on the rood loft; the altar furniture lay scattered on the floor, and the altar stone was covered in blood and dung. But this was not all. Also on the altar stone stood a neighbouring parson, wild with excitement, shouting at the top of his voice, and waving his arms about. When Skelton could make himself heard he inquired—in what manner one can easily imagine—what all this meant, and it then appeared that the intruder's hawks had pursued their prey, a dove, into the church, and were now in process of making a kill. Skelton, beside himself with anger, gave the 'lewde curate' a piece of his mind, but this served only to stimulate him to fresh insolence. He retorted that if he so desired he would bring not only his hawks but his hounds also into the church:

> He sayde he would not let
> His houndis for to fet,
> To hunte there by lyberte
> In the dyspyte of me,
> And to halow there the fox: ll. 106–110.

and to show his independence he immediately continued to shout and bawl at his hawks. Things got worse, and Skelton could apparently do nothing but stand aside and grind his teeth. Down came bell, book and candle; over with a crash went cross, staff, lectern, and banner. How it all ended we are not told, for Skelton breaks off suddenly at this point, dips his pen again in the ink, and prepares to curse the ribald from off the face of the earth.[1] It is a somewhat disappointing and lame conclusion.

The sporting parson is a familiar person; he had been a popular figure in literature for centuries before Skelton's time.[2] But this unworthy descendant of Chaucer's Monk is much worse than the usual type. It is difficult not to like the Monk, with his easy good-nature and genuine benevolence, but Skelton's visitor—tipsy, insolent, loud-mouthed, and callous—is another matter altogether:

> The hye auter he strypt naked;
> There on he stode, and craked;
> He shoke downe all the clothis,
> And sware horrible othes
> Before the face of God,
> By Moyses and Arons rod,
> Or that he thens yede,
> His hawke shoulde pray and fede
> Vpon a pigeons maw.
> The bloude ran downe raw
> Vpon the auter stone;
> The hawke tyrid on a bonne;
> And in the holy place
> She mutid there a chase
> Vpon my corporas face.
> Such *sacrificium laudis*
> He made with suche gambawdis.
>
> ll. 49–65.

The poet is bitterly angry. Not only had his personal feelings been completely ignored, but worse still, the Church herself, however absurdly, had been insulted, and he was as jealous of her honour as he was of his own. He was to say much more on this subject later, when the

[1] Dyce, I, pp. 155–166.
[2] See Gower, *Miroir de l'Omme*, ed. G. C. Macaulay, 1899, ll. 21043 *et seq;* *Vox Clamantis*, E.E.T.S. Bk. III, Cap. II, ll. 1505–10; Barclay, *The Ship of Fools*, ed. Jamieson, 1873, p. 220.

72

circumstances were far from ludicrous, and the 'losels' he was attacking far more insidious and formidable than an illiterate and boorish country parson. But here, in spite of his genuine indignation, Skelton cannot remain angry for very long. Cheerfulness will keep breaking in. *Ware the Hauke* recalls *Elynour Rummynge* in much of its capital fooling. The vigour and bravura of the style, the quaintness of the language, and the swing of the verse take a good deal of the edge from his anger. It is impossible not to smile at the eagerness with which he hurls his curses, and at the solemnity with which he halts at one point to give an entirely unnecessary disquisition on the habits of hawks:

> His seconde hawke wexid gery,
> And was with flying wery;
> She had flowin so oft,
> That on the rode loft
> She perkyd her to rest.
> The fauconer then was prest,
> Came runnyng with a dow,
> And cryed, Stow, stow, stow!
> But she would not bow.
> He then, to be sure,
> Callid her with a lure.
> Her mete was very crude,
> She had not wel endude;
> She was not clene ensaymed,
> She was not well reclaymed:
> But the fawconer vnfayned
> Was much more febler brayned.
>
> ll. 66–82.

Skelton evidently knew more than a little about hawking:[1] this is not the only poem in which he introduces terms connected with the sport. He was probably something of a sporting parson himself: we are informed more than

[1] As most people did. An almost contemporary enthusiast, John Paston, writes home to his brother in 1472: 'No more, but I pray God send you all your desyrs, and me my mwyd gosshawk in hast, or rather then fayle, a sowyr hawke.' *The Paston Letters*, ed. J. Gairdner, 1895, III, p. 56.

73

once that he knew a good deal about horses. But conduct such as he had witnessed within the very walls of his own church ran clean contrary to all his ideas of decorum and fitness; and when he is not clowning he is speaking from his heart. For the first time in his life he is writing more in sorrow than in anger.

Great display is made of things Biblical and Classical as he goes along. Skelton refers his enemy to 'Exedos,' and touches upon the subject of expiation for pollution of the Temple. In the inevitable catalogue the 'lewde curate' is compared, to his great disadvantage, with a long list of tyrants, ranging from Diocletian to 'Zorobabell':

> Of no tyrande I rede,
> That so farre dyd excede;
> Neyther yet Dioclesyan,
> Nor yet Domisian,
> Nor yet croked Cacus,
> Nor yet dronken Bacus;
> Nother Olibrius,
> Nor Dionisyus;
> Nother Phalary,
> Rehersed in Valery;
> Nor Sardanapall,
> Vnhappiest of all;
> Nor Nero the worst,
> Nor Clawdius the curst;
> Nor yet Egeas,
> Nor yet Syr Pherumbras;
> Nother Zorobabell;
> Nor cruel Jesabell;
> Nor yet Tarquinius,
> Whom Tytus Liuius
> In wrytynge doth enroll;
> I haue red them poll by poll; . . .

ll. 190–211.

It is interesting also to see in this poem the first appearance of those amazing conundrums which Skelton, true

74

to the fifteenth century delight in mystification, is fond of inserting into his later poems. He calls this one a 'tabull playne,' but so far it has eluded all attempts at solution. The offending parson was himself mystified, and declared, not unnaturally, that

> . . . for a crokid intent
> The wordes were paruerted:

'paruerted' they have remained.

As far as structure and technical excellence are concerned there is nothing new in the poem. Beyond affording the reader a further glimpse into Skelton's personal feelings and command of diatribe it has little to offer: certainly nothing to the lover of poetry. But it marks a turning point in Skelton's career. The Church, however feebly, has been assailed. Skelton has been compelled to review the present state of the clergy, and to ask himself what will be the end of the matter.

CHAPTER VII

'MAGNYFYCENCE'

SINCE *The Bowge of Courte* Skelton had done nothing
to enhance his reputation as a poet: indeed in some
quarters he had by now forfeited all claims to consideration. But he himself was not perturbed in any way,
and for a very good reason. His view was that poets are
created by God: once a poet always a poet. As one of
these chosen vessels he had nothing to fear, and his own
opinion of his merits never wavered in the least. But he
was not a fool, and he would certainly not have claimed
Divine inspiration for *Elynour Rummynge*. Indeed it is
more than likely that he had a sneaking sympathy with
those who refused to regard such things as poetry at all.
For whenever he addresses an audience of noble and
discreet persons on a subject of importance he returns to
the 'high style' with which he had made his reputation.
Thus *Magnyfycence*,[1] his only extant play, is dignified and
weighty: aureate and polished terms abound. For it is a
warning to the King, his old pupil; and Kings cannot be
addressed in Skeltonics. So the academic in Skelton comes
uppermost once again, and for a time it is as though
Elynour had never been. For all that, *Magnyfycence* is a
tragedy in more than one sense. Thalia often nods, but it
is hard to forgive her for not inspiring Skelton to write
the first native English comedy. Everything lay ready to
hand: vigour and exuberance, knowledge of men and
manners, mastery of language, humour. The play which,
as far as we know, Skelton did not write, could hardly
have been subtle, but it would have been extremely enter-

[1] Dyce, I, pp. 225–310. See Dr. R. L. Ramsay's exhaustive and stimulating
edition of the play, to which I am greatly indebted. Another play, *A New
Enterlude of Godly Queene Hester*, ed. W. W. Greg, *Materielen zur Kunde des alteren
Englischen Dramas*, B. 5, 1904, has been tentatively attributed to Skelton. See also
Ramsay, *op. cit.*, cxvi. But I cannot convince myself that Skelton had anything
to do with it.

taining. Instead of such a play, however, we have to be content with *Magnyfycence*, 'A goodly interlude and a mery, deuysed and made by Mayster Skelton, Poet Laureate.' It is true that this was not his only play. We hear in *The Garlande of Laurell* of

His commedy, Achademios callyd by name,

and

Of Vertu also the souerayne interlude.

These, however, were probably examples of the academic Latin play on the lines of those performed at the Inns of Court. He also mentions a work entitled *Diologgis of Imagynacyoun*, and these also may have been cast into dramatic form. No trace however of these works has survived.

Joseph Warton claimed to have seen a copy of yet another play, printed by Wynkyn de Worde in 1504:

The Nigramansir, a morell Enterlude and a pithie, written by Maister Skelton laureate and plaid before the King and other estatys at Woodstoke on Palme Sunday.

This copy, according to Warton, belonged to William Collins, and was lost when Collins died and his books were dispersed.[1] He gives a full description of the play:

The characters are a Necromancer or conjurer, the devil, a notary public, Simonie, and Philargyria or Avarice. It is partly a satire on some abuses in the church: yet not without a due regard to decency and an apparent respect for the dignity of the audience. The story, or plot, is the tryal of SIMONY and AVARICE: the devil is the judge, and the notary public acts as an assessor or scribe. The prisoners, as we may suppose, are found guilty, and ordered into hell immediately. There is no sort of propriety in calling this play the Necromancer: for the only business and use of this character, is to open the subject in a long prologue, to evoke the devil,

---

[1] ' My lamented friend Mr. William Collins, whose odes will be remembered while any taste for true poetry remains, shewed me this piece at Chichester, not many years before his death: and he pointed it out as a very rare and valuable curiosity.' *History of English Poetry*, ed. 1870, pp. 557–558; Dyce, I, xcix–c.

and to summon the court. The devil kicks the necromancer, for waking him so soon in the morning: a proof that this drama was performed in the morning, perhaps in the chapel of the palace. A variety of measures, with shreds of Latin and French, is used, but the devil speaks in the octave stanza. One of the stage-directions is, *Enter Balsebub with a Berde* . . . Philargyria quotes Seneca and saint Austin: and Simony offers the devil a bribe. The devil rejects her offer with much indignation: and swears by the *foule Eumenides*, and the hoary beard of Charon, that she shall be well fried and roasted in the unfathomable sulphur of Cocytus, together with Mahomet, Pontius Pilate, the traitor Judas, and King Herod. The last scene is closed with a view of hell, and a dance between the devil and the necromancer. The dance ended, the devil trips up the necromancer's heels, and disappears in fire and smoke.

Unless Warton has manufactured an elaborate hoax—and there is no reason to suppose anything of the kind—such a play evidently once existed, and Skelton's name appeared on the title page. As we have seen, there is no mention of it in *The Garlande of Laurell*, and as this solitary exemplar of the play is apparently lost for ever, further speculation as to its nature is obviously useless. Warton's description is not unlike what one may imagine Skelton's conception of comedy to have been. It is unfortunate that there is no corroborative evidence.

There is no extant record of any production of a play by Skelton, but from the context it seems likely that *Magnyfycence* was at some time performed before the 'Kynge and other estatys.' If the possibility of a royal audience is eliminated, a good deal of the significance of the play vanishes at once. Its content is topical matter, like that of *The Bowge of Courte*, and Skelton's object is to show in the similitude of a dream the dangers which beset the King and his realm. It is thus a mixture of abstract and particular elements. Magnyfycence himself is both Henry VIII and a personification of a weak-minded spendthrift, and the other characters, though they probably do not represent actual personalities at court, are yet designed as an epitome of the general characteristics of a party or an individual courtier. The evil counsellors of Magnyfycence have a direct reference to the party of young and extravagant favourites headed by Wolsey: the sober and cautious group represents the old nobility under the guidance of the Duke of Norfolk.

The story of the play concerns the ruin of a great prince by his false friends, and his restoration after repentance and shame. Since in 1516, when the play was probably written, Wolsey and his supporters were by no means at the height of their power and influence, the play is not primarily designed as a mirror of contemporary events. It is rather a grave warning. Skelton lays bare the root of the trouble, and foreshadows what will come about if the disease is not checked in good time. The play thus falls directly into line with the satires, and contains in embryo most of the criticism which Skelton was to clarify and elaborate later. *Magnyfycence* is his first shot in a campaign against the Cardinal which was to end in sanctuary at Westminster thirteen years afterwards.

The political situation at the time must be briefly glanced at. In 1513 Henry VIII prepared to invade the North of France, hoping to remedy the humiliation which had been the result of the Guienne expedition in the previous year, when England's first attempt for some time to assert herself on the continent had ignominiously collapsed. Wolsey strained every nerve to bring about the success of the new venture, and exhibited an administrative genius which impressed the King greatly. 'Nothing was too trivial for his attention even down to beer barrels and biscuits.' The English army landed safely at Calais, and after some little time Terouenne surrendered, and Henry went on to reduce Tournai. In spite of the eagerness of Maximilian, who had brought a small contingent of Germans and had flattered Henry's vanity by pretend-

ing to fight under his leadership, Henry departed for
England before the winter, to find that a far greater
victory had been won at home in his absence. The Scots,
taking advantage of the unprepared state of the country,
had invaded England and been annihilated at Flodden.
Henry himself had done nothing but satisfy, at great
expense, his own vanity.

In 1514 Wolsey arranged an alliance between the
Princess Mary and the old King of France, Louis XII.
This brilliant piece of diplomacy made England the envy
of Europe. Both Ferdinand and Maximilian realized at
once that England, or more correctly Wolsey, was a
force to be reckoned with. Unfortunately, however,
Louis XII soon died, on January 1, 1515. His death was a
severe rebuff for Wolsey. The alliance had been unpopu-
lar at home, and the Duke of Norfolk and the conservatives had seen in it a further example of his growing
power. It seemed as if an opportunity of displacing him
had now arrived, but in spite of innumerable disappoint-
ments he kept his hold on Henry's affections, and brought
his foreign policy to a triumphant conclusion by the
universal peace of 1518. Skelton alludes to Louis XII
early in the play:

FANSY.   Largesse is he that all prynces doth auaunce
            I reporte me herein to Kynge Lewes of Fraunce.
FELYCYTE. Why haue he hym named, and all other refused?
FANSY.   For, syth he dyed, Largesse was lytell vsed.
                                 ll. 282–285.

The play therefore cannot have been written before 1515:
it is impossible to imagine that this passage refers to
Louis XI.

As Dr. Ramsay points out,[1] it seems strange at first
that Louis XII should be commended for liberality in
preference to the brilliant Francis I, but Skelton is writing
in the midst of the negotiations over Princess Mary's

[1] *Op. cit.*, xxii.

dowry. 'The same jewels which had been so lavishly bestowed upon the royal bride now formed the subject of a long and intricate negotiation, in the conduct of which Mary's happiness and the obligations of 'largesse' were alike forgotten by both Henry and Francis. "In a fit of stinginess, more befitting his father, Henry demanded the restoration of Mary's jewels and furniture; all the expenses of her passage were to be returned, and the sums reimbursed that had been laid out in providing her bridal apparel."

Not unnaturally the French objected. The negotiations were daily more complicated and embittered; "the generous spirit in which they had been commenced was fast disappearing, and was superseded by the less amiable desire of each party to outwit and overreach the other." [1]

A further passage seems to point to hostility with France. When Fansy produces his counterfeit letter he expatiates on his harassing experiences 'at the see syde':

MAGN. Where was it delyuered you? shewe vnto me.
FAN. By God, Syr, beyonde the se.
MAGN. At what place, nowe, as you gesse?
FAN. By my trouthe, syr, at Pountesse;
This wrytynge was taken me there,
But neuer was I in gretter fere.
MAGN. Howe so?
FAN. By God, at the see syde,
Had I not opened my purse wyde,
I trowe, by our lady, I had ben slayne,
Or elles I had lost myne eres twayne.
MAGN. By your soth?
FAN. Ye, and there is suche a wache,
That no man can escape but they hym cache.
They bare me in hande that I was a spye;
And another bade put out myne eye,
Another wolde myne eye were blerde,
Another bade shaue halfe my berde;

---

[1] Ramsay, *op. cit.*, xxiv. The quotations are from Brewer, *The reign of Henry VIII from his accession to the death of Wolsey*, 1884, I, p. 85.

And boyes to the pylery gan me plucke,
And wolde haue made me Freer Tucke,
To preche out of the pylery hole,
Without an antetyme or a stole;
And some bade sere hym with a marke:
To gete me fro them I had moche warke.

ll. 343-366.

Negotiations for peace, however, began in 1516, and the latest date for the composition of the play must be 1518, when Princess Mary was betrothed to Francis; it was probably written in 1516, the date of the Treaty of Noyon.

Magnyfycence, as we have suggested, is like Skelton's earlier work and unlike the Wolsey poems in that it contains few hints of open war. The allusions, though numerous, are always adequately protected by their accompanying moral significance. The six vices, Fansy, Counterfet Countenaunce, Crafty Conueyaunce, Clokyd Colusyon, Courtly Abusyon and Foly, though they can easily be made to apply to various aspects of Wolsey's character, are familiar types, and of the kith and kin of the rogues in *The Bowge of Courte*. This double aspect of the play lends it a peculiar interest, since it is not only important as a new kind of Morality, but is also a valuable social document, containing the views of the moderate party at Court and abroad during the earlier period of Wolsey's ascendancy.

Skelton was evidently very anxious that his old pupil, of whom even in his most despondent moments he speaks with affection and respect, should not fall into the pit which he clearly saw was being digged for him. *Magnyfycence* is an appeal as well as an entertainment. Years before, Skelton had compiled a manual for his pupil's guidance: now 'as the old tutor of Henry he doubtless felt privileged to follow his pupil's career with something of his former authority. *Magnyfycence* must have seemed to the King, if he ever saw the play, like a reminiscence of his school-days.' But Skelton was soon to see, to his great bitterness, that his lesson had produced no effect.

At any rate he had made a great effort. This play is his largest and most ambitious performance. It contains over two thousand five hundred lines, and shows much evidence of careful thought and preparation. It is distinguished from other and earlier Moralities in that it strikes a mean between the old and the new, by marking the transition from moral play to secular allegory; by exhibiting considerable structural originality in the plot; and by the introduction of new measures and a careful adaptation of the old. There is nothing surprising in this. In *The Bowge of Courte* he had done very much the same thing on a smaller and less elaborate scale. He had utilized the Court allegory for his own purposes and changed its nature in the process. In *Magnyfycence* he moulds the moral play to these purposes and achieves a similar result.

It cannot be admitted however that the play holds the attention. One would not be at all surprised to hear that its reception by the King was similar to that which was accorded to a play of Medwall's, when

> The kynge roos up and departed to his chamber.

There is very little action, and the central figure of the play is hardly convincing: indeed the whole characterization is somewhat feeble. The most vivid moments are supplied by the rogues, who sing on occasion, and possess a deep and varied acquaintance with the murkier side of London life. When they appear a little life creeps into the play, but for the greater part of it Skelton seems to be hampered by the dignity of his subject and his audience. Here he is very much the Laureate. Apart from the scenes of low life, the play in fact possesses little but academic interest. This however is so considerable that it is worthy of further examination.

In the first place the *décor* is ostensibly the traditional allegorical setting: the language is full of 'polished and covert terms,' and Skelton invents new names for many of the old figures. Dr. Ramsay has pointed out that their force is not always easy to grasp 'even when they are put beside their traditional predecessors,' but it is clear that save in the case of Measure, Dyspare, Aduersyte and Pouerte, who are new allegorical figures, the conception remains fundamentally the same. The language of the play, or at any rate the greater part of it, is rather stilted than dignified:

> To tell you the cause me semeth it no nede,
> The amense therof is far to call agayne;
> For, when men by welth, they haue lytyll drede
> Of that may come after; experyence trewe and playne,
> Howe after a drought there fallyth a showre of rayne,
> And after a hete oft cometh a stormy colde.
> A man may haue welth, but not, as he wolde,
> Ay to contynewe and styll to endure;
> But yf prudence be proued with sad cyrcumspeccyon,
> Welthe myght be wonne and made to the lure,
> Yf noblenesse were aquayntyd with sober dyreccyon;
> But wyll hath reason so vnder subieccyon,
> And so dysordereth this worlde ouer all,
> That welthe and felicite is passynge small.
>
> ll. 8–21.

The satirical matter of the play, however, is cleverly handled, and full use is made of the protection afforded by the allegorical form. Magnyfycence himself is always treated with respect, though the inevitable results of his actions are remorselessly carried to their conclusion. He is exhibited as a generous and noble-spirited prince, whose downfall is mainly the fault of crafty counsellors, who take advantage of his pride and conceit and bring him to ruin. All this can be applied to the situation in 1516, when Henry had spent an enormous amount of money in subsidizing Maximilian and the Swiss for the Milan fiasco. Wolsey does not appear as a single personage. His character is sub-divided among the six vices, each of whom affords the dramatist an opportunity for

enlarging upon some particular defect in Wolsey's
actions and character. Nothing is openly displayed, but it
is noticeable that precisely the same criticisms appear
later, couched in very much more indecorous language
and clearly addressed to Wolsey. Here the evidence for
their application to him rests on the closeness with which
the criticisms fit what we know to have been Skelton's
estimate of the various shades of his character. The
following speech of Counterfet Countenaunce reads very
familiarly to anyone acquainted with the later satires:

> A knokylbonyarde wyll counterfet a clarke,
> He wolde trotte gentylly, but he is to starke,
> At his cloked counterfetynge dogges dothe barke;
> A carter a courtyer, it is a worthy warke,
> That with his whyp his mares was wonte to yarke;
> A custrell to dryue the deuyll out of the derke,
> A counterfet courtyer with a knaues marke.
> To counterfet this freers haue lerned me;
> This nonnes nowe and then, and it myght be,
> Wolde take, in the way of counterfet charyte,
> The grace of God vnder *benedicite*;
> To counterfet thyr counsell they gyue me a fee;
> Chanons can not counterfet but vpon thre,
> Monkys may not for drede that men sholde them se.
>
> ll. 485–498.

Skelton's new importations into the usual satiric material
are moreover for the most part used as vehicles for
criticism of Wolsey alone. Counterfet Countenaunce,
for instance, jeers at base birth, and the rake Courtly
Abusyon is especially distinguished for his ostentatious
dress, a fact which connects him at once with the Cardinal.
Wolsey too is represented as primarily responsible for the
ruin of Magnyfycence. Other persons may perhaps be
glanced at for a moment, but such references are rare,
and carry little weight in comparison with the exposure
and denunciation of the leading spirit of the opposition.

JOHN SKELTON

It is noticeable that Skelton himself inclines towards
the spirit of caution and moderation, for his characterization of the spendthrift party is much more detailed than
that of the conservatives. In other circumstances this
might well have been considered as an example of Skelton's predilection for rascality, but in *Magnyfycence* he
has a point to prove, and he hopes to drive his message
home by laying bare the scandal in great detail.

Measure and Cyrcumspeccyon embody the spirit of
Henry VII, then represented by the Duke of Norfolk and
his party. It may be added that although Skelton was no
doubt quite aware of this, he cannot have failed to realize
the far greater dramatic value of the evil councillors:
caution and husbandry are not good subjects for a play,
moral or otherwise. At any rate he lavishes the whole
of his resources upon the portrayal of the infinitely more
fascinating rogues and rascals. These figures are certainly
very much more elaborate than those of *The Bowge of
Courte*, but unfortunately they gain very little from the
greater detail. It is much easier to obtain a coherent
mental picture of Haruy Hafter or Ryotte than of Fansy
or Foly, for Skelton does not attempt a rapid character
study of these latter, and their talk is generally so incoherent that a clear picture is hard to come at. For all that
there is a great similarity between the conversation of all
of them. The following speech of Fansy to the King
might easily have come from the earlier poem:

> Plucke up your mynde, syr; what ayle you to muse?
>   Haue ye not welthe here at your wyll?
> It is but a maddynge, these wayes that ye vse:
>   What auayleth lordshyp, yourselfe for to kyll
>   With care and with thought howe Jacke shall haue Gyl?
> ll. 286–290.

These vagabonds indeed have a strong air of verisimili-
tude under their allegorical dress, and their language and
habits are drawn from Skelton's observation of contem-

porary life in the London streets. This localization is
important. As in *The Bowge of Courte* Skelton had sub-
stituted Harwich Port for a more nebulous background,
so here, though there is no definite statement about the
scene of the play, the whole setting is furnished from
actual concrete elements. It is moreover possible to see
in the vices all the elements which had gone to make up
Skelton's earlier poems. This song of Lyberte is directly
in the style of *Lullay, lullay*:

> With, ye mary, syrs, thus sholde it be.
> I kyst her swete, and she kyssyd me;
> I daunsed the darlynge on my kne;
> I garde her gaspe, I garde her gle,
> With, daunce on the le, the le!
> I bassed that baby with harte so free;
>   She is the bote of all my bale:
> A, so, that syghe was farre fet!
> To loue that louesome I wyll not let;
> My harte is holly on her set:
> I plucked her by the patlet;
> At my deuyse I with her met;
> My fansy fayrly on her I set;
>   So merely syngeth the nyghtyngale!

ll. 2090–2103.

The reader is forcibly reminded on several occasions of
Elynour Rummynge and *Ware the Hauke*. Indeed, Skelton
refers to hawking more elaborately than ever before.
Fansy discourses in learned fashion on this topic:

> Stowe, byrde, stowe, stowe!
> It is best I fede my hawke now.
> There is many euyll faueryd, and thou be foule;
> Eche thynge is fayre when it is yonge: all hayle, owle!
> Lo, this is
> My fansy, I wys;
> Nowe Cryst it blysse!
> It is, by Jesse,
> A byrde full swete,

87

For me full mete:
She is furred for the hete
All to the fete;
Her browys bent,
Her eyen glent:
Frome Tyne to Trent,
From Stroude to Kent,
A man shall fynde
Many of her kynde,
Howe standeth the wynde,
Before or behynde: . . .

ll. 980–999.

This is far from allegory, and a great relief from political
moralizing. It must be noticed, moreover, that side by side
with the political satire there is also a vast quantity of
social documentation which is of far greater interest to
the modern reader. It is strange that this has not been
more clearly pointed out, for together with the vigour
and exuberance of the scenes of lowlife, and the occasional
dignity and impressiveness of the monologues, it provides
the most abiding interest and chief value of the play.

These observations are naturally put into the mouths
of the vices, and expressed with all Skelton's directness
and force. Here for example is an account of contemporary society put into the mouth of Counterfet Countenaunce:

Counterfet maters in the lawe of the lande,
Wyth golde and grotes they grese my hande,
In stede of ryght that wronge may stande,
And counterfet fredome that is bounde;
I counterfet suger that is but sande;
Counterfet capytaynes by me are mande;
Of all lewdnesse I kyndell the brande;
Counterfet kyndnesse, and thynke dyscayte;
Counterfet letters by the way of sleyght;
Subtelly vsynge counterfet weyght;
Counterfet langage, fayty bone geyte.
Counterfetynge is a proper bayte;

A courte to counterfet in a resayte;
To counterfet well is a good consayte.
Counterfet maydenhode may well be borne,
But counterfet coynes is laughynge to scorne;
It is euyll patchynge of that is torne;
When the noppe is rughe, it wolde be shorne;
Counterfet haltynge without a thorne;
Yet counterfet chafer is but euyll corne;
All thynge is worse whan it is worne.
What, wolde ye, wyues, counterfet
The courtly gyse of the newe iet?
An olde barne wolde be vnderset:
It is moche worthe that is ferre fet.
What, wanton, wanton, nowe well ymet!
What, Margery Mylke Ducke, mermoset!
It wolde be masked in my net;
It wolde be nyce, thoughe I say nay;
By Crede, it wolde haue fresshe aray,
And therfore shall my husbande pay;
To counterfet she wyll assay
All the newe gyse, fresshe and gaye,
And be as praty as she may,
And iet it ioly as a iay: . . .   ll. 436–470.

At line 755 we are back again in the ale house; it would
not be in the least surprising to see Elynour Rummynge
come in through the open door:

COURT. AB. Huffa, huffa, taunderum, taunderum, tayne,
    huffa, huffa!
CL. COL. This was properly prated, syrs! what sayd a?
COURT. AB. Rutty bully, ioly rutterkyn, heyda!
CL. COL. *De que pays este vous?*
     Et faciat tanquam exuat barretum ironice.
COURT. AB. Decke your hofte and couer a lowce.
CL. COL. *Say vous chaunter Venter tre dawce?*
COURT. AB. *Wyda, wyda.*
    Howe sayst thou, man? am not I a ioly
    rutter?
CL. COL. Gyue this gentylman rome, syrs, stonde vtter!
         ll. 755–763.

JOHN SKELTON

It is interesting to see that Miles Gloriosus is still walking the streets:

COURT. AB. Cockes bones, I ne tell can
     Whiche of you is the better man,
     Or whiche of you can do most.
CR. CON. In fayth, I rule moche of the rost.
CL. COL. Rule the roste! thou woldest, ye?
     As skante thou had no nede of me.
CR. CON. Nede! yes, mary, I say not nay.
COURT.AB. Cockes harte, I trowe thou wylte make a fray.
CR. CON. Nay, in good faythe, it is but the gyse.
CL. COL. No, for, or we stryke, we wyll be aduysed
     twyse.
COURT. AB. What the deuyll, vse ye not to drawe no
     swordes?
CR. CON. No, by my trouthe, but crake grete wordes.
COURT. AB. Why, is this the gyse nowe adayes?
CL. COL. Ye, for surety, ofte peas is taken for frayes.
     But, syr, I wyll haue this man with me.
            ll. 810–824.

At one point Courtly Abusyon delivers a homily on modern fashions:

COURT. AB. What nowe, let se,
     Who loketh on me
     Well rounde aboute,
     Howe gay and howe stoute
     That I can were
     Courtly my gere:
     My heyre bussheth
     So plesauntly,
     My robe russheth
     So ruttyngly,
     Me seme I flye,
     I am so lyght,
     To daunce delyght;
     Properly drest,
     All poynte deuyse,
     My persone prest
     Beyonde all syse

'MAGNYFYCENCE'

Of the newe gyse,
To russhe it oute
In euery route:
Beyonde measure
My sleue is wyde,
Al of pleasure
My hose strayte tyde,
My buskyn wyde,
Ryche to beholde,
Gletterynge in golde.

ll. 838–864.

Boar-hunting is alluded to in an amusing dialogue between Fansy and Foly:

FAN. What callest thou thy dogge?
FOL.   Tusshe, his name is Gryme.
FAN. Come, Gryme, come, Gryme! it is my praty dogges.
FOL. In faythe, there is not a better dogge for hogges,
     Not from Anwyke vnto Aungey.

ll. 1132–1136.

At line 1253 Foly enumerates, somewhat in the manner of Puck but with nothing of his grace, a few of the people he delights in tormenting:

Ye, by God, syr, for a nede,
I haue another maner of sorte,
That I laugh at for my dysporte;
And those be they that come vp of nought,
As some be not ferre, and yf it were well sought:
Suche dawys, what soeuer they be,
That be set in auctorite,
Anone he waxyth so hy and prowde,
He frownyth fyersly, brymly browde,
The knaue wolde make it koy, and he cowde;
All that he dothe, muste be alowde;
And, This is not well done, syr, take hede;
And maketh hym besy where is no nede:
He dawnsys so long, hey, troly loly,
That euery man lawghyth at his foly.

ll. 1253–1267.

91

JOHN SKELTON

The temporary overthrow and disgrace of Magnyfycence gives Skelton an excellent opportunity of pointing out the great difference between rich and poor in Tudor England:

MAGN. Alas, of Fortune I may well complayne!
POUER. Ye, syr, yesterday wyll not be callyd agayne:
     But yet, syr, nowe in this case,
     Take it mekely, and thanke God of his grace;
     For nowe go I wyll begge for you some mete:
     It is foly agaynst God for to plete;
     I wyll walke nowe with my beggers baggys,
     And happe you the whyles with these homly raggys.
     A, howe my lymmys be lyther and lame!
     Better it is to begge than to be hangyd with shame;
     Yet many had leuer hangyd to be,
     Then for to begge theyr mete for charyte:
     They thynke it no shame to robbe and stele,
     Yet were they better to begge, a great dele;
     For by robbynge they rynne to *in manus tuas* quecke,
     But beggynge is better medecyne for the necke;
     Ye, mary, is it, ye, so mote I goo:
     A Lorde God, howe the gowte wryngeth me by the too!

                      ll. 2056–2073.

Frequent specific local references are a feature of the play, and these provide a particularly vivid background to the scene. Courtly Abusyon's cryptic reference to the person 'brought up of nought' in line 908 ends with the prophecy

     A Tyborne checke
     Shall breke his necke.

Crafty Conueyaunce refers in one place to the 'rode of Wodstoke Park' to give emphasis to his assertions: Lyberte, in a speech illustrating the abuses of power, alludes to those accursed creatures who

     fall prechynge at the Toure hyll.

Counterfet Countenaunce, bent on debauchery, summons his friends to the notorious 'halfe-strete'; and, predicting the end of those who are foolish enough to trust in him, refers once again to Tyburn:

> Thus at the laste I brynge hym ryght
> To Tyburne, where they hange on hyght.

It would be easy to multiply such examples, but enough has been quoted to make it clear that in this play, in spite of allegory and elegant language, in spite of the King and the great Estates of the realm, we have the boisterous living London of Skelton's time before our eyes. *Magnyfycence* is the product of both the laureate poet and the author of *Elynour Rummynge* and *Colyn Cloute*. Like *The Bowge of Courte* the play shows these two personalities working side by side, but more sharply separated from each other than in the earlier poems, and Skelton himself is far from being unconscious of the fact. The scenes of low life and depravity, and the language of the rascals, are designed to provide a contrast to the sober and dignified matters, to mark the difference between what is right and fitting and what is the product of immorality and deceit. But in spite of his high moral intent Skelton betrays his liking for his low folk, with all their vivacity and animal spirits, though he is, as always, perfectly comfortable in his chamber above-stairs.

There is singular novelty in the plot, though fundamentally it is the same as that of *The Castle of Perseverence* 'and of almost every other moral play which is extant from that date to its own.' The striking difference between the old and the new is that whereas previous moral plays had been exclusively concerned with prosperity after death, *Magnyfycence* is occupied first and foremost with the prosperity of this world. 'The basis of the play, accordingly, is no longer a theological but a philosophical allegory.'[1]

[1] Ramsay, *op. cit.*, lxxi.

JOHN SKELTON

It is impossible to doubt that this change in front was largely due to the circumstances under which the play was written. Satire is directed not vaguely at mankind in general, but at the follies and vices of a particular court: the hero of the play is not a typical man, but an actual embodiment of royalty. The canvas on which the dramatist works is thus considerably smaller, but there is no lack of detail, and the effect is certainly more concentrated and effective than usual. The source of the play may indeed be the *Speculum Principis*, though the suggestion is at best of doubtful value. Such ideas as those contained in *Magnyfycence* are not confined to royal text-books like Hoccleve's *Regement of Princes*. They had been in the air now for a very long time: they appear for instance in the pseudo-Aristotelian *Secreta Secretorum*, which Skelton may well have seen. The mere fact that there was a large number of extant works dealing with the subject is proof enough of its popularity and widespread circulation. The central conception of *Magnyfycence*, the gospel of the mean—the virtue of measure—is of course purely Aristotelian, and Skelton's studies at Cambridge probably put him in the way of much similar material.

The extreme technical ingenuity which Skelton exhibits throughout the play must now be briefly glanced at, for it is not only the result of a great deal of thought and labour, but remarkably successful into the bargain. Without attempting to confine himself to any rigid scheme, he continually varies his metre to suit the needs of characterization, and this required a great deal of careful adjustment. There is a noticeable contrast for instance between the verse of the first six scenes of the play, which are chiefly concerned with the dignified Magnyfycence, Felycyte and Measure, and the seventh, in which the mercurial Fansy begins to gain a firm hold on the King's affections. The rhymed native long-line of four stresses is used throughout the play to illustrate themes of

94

importance and dignity, and it naturally appears in these
preliminary scenes:

> Oracius to recorde, in his volumys olde,
> With euery condycyon measure must be sought:
> Welthe without measure wolde bere hymselfe to bolde,
> Lyberte without measure proue a thynge of nought;
> I ponder by nomber, by measure all thynge is wrought,
> As at the fyrst orygynall by godly opynyon;
> Whych prouyth well that measure shold have domynyon: ..
>
> ll. 115–121.

The four-foot line which is used by Fansy is a much
slighter thing: the frequent omission of the caesura robs
it of a great deal of the dignity of the more sober line:

> Measure is mete for a marchauntes hall,
> But largesse becometh a state ryall.
> What, sholde you pynche at a pecke of otes,
> Ye wolde sone pynche at a pecke of grotes.
> Thus is the talkynge of one and of oder,
> As men dare speke it hugger mugger;
> A lorde a negarde, it is a shame,
> But Largesse may amende your name.
>
> ll. 387–394.

The scenes in which the rascals argue among themselves
are similarly distinguished: the lines are full of dramatic
colour, and provide a very effective contrast to the verse
of the slower and weightier scenes:

> C. Count. What is Largesse without Lyberte?
> Cr. Con. By Mesure mastered yet is he.
> C. Count. What, is your conueyaunce no better?
> Fan.   In faythe, Mesure is lyke a tetter,
>   That ouergroweth a mannes face,
>   So he ruleth ouer all our place.
> Cr. Con. Nowe therfore, whylest we are togyder,—
>   Counterfet Countenaunce, nay, come hyder,—
>   I say, whylest we are togyder in same—
> C. Count. Tushe, a straw, it is a shame
>   That we can no better than so.
>
> ll. 546–556.

JOHN SKELTON

It is not surprising to see Skelton making great use of
alliteration to heighten the effect of impressive passages
such as the following great speech of Aduersyte, one of
the most memorable in the play:

I am Aduersyte, that for thy mysdede
From God am sent to quyte thé thy mede.
Vyle velyarde, thou must not nowe my dynt withstande,
Thou must now abyde the dynt of my hande:
Ly there, losell for all thy pompe and pryde;
Thy pleasure now with payne and trouble shalbe tryde.
The stroke of God, Aduersyte I hyght;
I pluke downe kynge, prynce, lorde, and knyght,
I rushe at them rughly, and make them ly full lowe,
And in theyr moste truste I make them ouerthrowe.
Thys losyll was a lorde, and lyuyd at his lust,
And nowe, lyke a lurden, he lyeth in the duste:
He knewe not hymselfe, his harte was so hye;
Nowe is there no man that wyll set by hym a flye:
He was wonte to boste, brage, and to brace;
Nowe dare he not for shame loke one in the face:
All worldly welth for hym to lytell was;
Nowe hath he ryght nought, naked as an asse:
Somtyme without measure he trusted in golde,
And now without mesure he shal haue hunger and colde.
Lo, syrs, thus I handell them all
That folowe theyr fansyes in foly to fall:
Man or woman, of what estate they be,
I counsayle them beware of Aduersyte.
Of sorowfull seruantes I haue many scores:
I vysyte them somtyme with blaynes and with sores;
With botches and carbuckyls in care I them knyt;
With the gowte I make them to grone where they syt;
Some I make lyppers and lazars full horse;
And from that they loue best some I deuorse;
Some with the marmoll to halte I them make;
And some to cry out of the bone ake; . . . .

ll. 1902–2933.

Alliteration is also employed to create an effect of vaunting in boastful talk:

96

'MAGNYFYCENCE'

Of Cato the counte, accountyd the cane,
    Daryus, the doughty cheftayn of Perse,
I set not by the prowdest of them a prane,
    Ne by non other than any man can rehersse.
I folowe in felycyte without reuersse,
    I drede no daunger, I dawnce all in delyte;
    My name is Magnyfycence, man most of myght.

                ll. 1505–1511.

As we have already seen, something like Skelton's own favourite metre also makes an appearance:

A very fon,
A very asse,
Wyll take vpon
To compasse
That neuer was
Abusyd before;
A very pore
That so wyll do,
He doth abuse
Hym selfe to to;
He dothe mysse vse
Eche man to akuse,
To crake and prate;
I befoule his pate.

                ll. 872–885.

These are but a few points; Skelton's skill and resource deserve much more illustration than is possible here. *Magnyfycence*, possessing 'so rich a scale of metrical variations, far richer than any other morality can boast,' is a storehouse of examples of Skelton's employment of his vast technique—the only single work of his in which it can be studied with anything like completeness. And the play also helps the reader to understand why Skelton himself had so high an opinion of his poetic powers. A virtuoso is surely entitled to indulge occasionally in a little display of vanity, and this work is an exhibition of supreme craftsmanship. Regarded simply as a piece of academic writing, *Magnyfycence* is his finest

H   97

work. Much was at stake, and he threw everything he knew into the play. He had worked hard at his warning, though what he has to say is for the most part wrapped up in a more or less decorous fashion. But one thing at any rate is clear: he has made up his mind and come once and for all to a definite conclusion. In *Magnyfycence* he has been addressing, possibly to their very faces, the great ones of the realm. He has spoken to his old pupil as plainly as he dares, and it has been impossible, under the circumstances, to go further; in that direction at least he can do no more. He has declared his purpose through the old traditional channels—the court must be warned in courtly fashion—but now he leaves the court behind him and goes out into the street. The people, misguided and deluded, shall hear what he has in mind. He must have realized very well what he was about to do: that when he put pen to paper in this new fashion he might be signing his own death-warrant. He does not, it is true, at any time disdain attempts at disguise, but he must have known that they were at best a woefully thin covering. Even the least acute of his hearers could not doubt his meaning for a moment, and Wolsey's ears were very quick indeed. Skelton was probably somewhere about sixty when he began his mission, and he went on until death stopped him. By that time, however, he had said all he had to say.

CHAPTER VIII

THE SATIRES

I

THE WOLSEY POEMS

IT is impossible to say exactly when Skelton began his great campaign against the Cardinal, but it is clear from the allusions in *Magnyfycence* that he had been turning such a project over in his mind for some years before 1518. It is possible that a new quarrel with Wolsey (or the recrudescence of an old enmity) brought matters to a head, but there is no evidence to be had on this point. The incoherent fury of his attack on Wolsey in *Why come ye nat to Courte?* is perhaps difficult to account for on other than personal grounds. But at any rate it is certain that at some time not later than 1518 Skelton found that he could contain himself no longer, and began his long and bitter survey of the state of the realm in general and the shortcomings of Wolsey in particular.

The three poems which form this survey, *Speke Parrot*, *Colyn Cloute* and *Why come ye nat to Courte?*[1] are on the whole a little disappointing. *Colyn Cloute*, which is the best of them, will no doubt always be read and admired, for it is a fine piece of writing, English to the core and full of vitality, but the incoherence of much of *Speke Parrot* and the hysteria of *Why Come ye nat to Courte?* try the patience. Indeed some of Skelton's worst faults appear in an intensified form in these poems. He is garrulous; he finds it hard to weigh a situation critically and calmly; and he says the first thing that comes into his

---

[1] Possibly all written between 1521 and 1522, though the question is full of difficulties. See William Nelson, *P.M.L.A.*, March 1936, pp. 59–82; June 1936, pp. 377–98; June 1938, pp. 601–22 (with H. L. R. Edwards); Berdan, *op. cit.*, pp. 175–7; Brie, *loc. cit.*

head. And yet, curiously enough, he is perhaps more entertaining here than anywhere else in his works. Enthusiasm such as his is infectious, and to a poet who is not dull one may legitimately allow a very great deal of latitude. For his surprising vigour is not only undiminished but seems rather to have increased with the passage of years: the force and drive of his verse and the delightful virtuosity with which fine words are scattered abroad were never more clearly in evidence. Moreover it must be admitted that much of the obscurity—that of *Speke Parrot* for example—may be due to modern ignorance of the finer details of the situation. It is certain that some of it was strategically necessary.

For all that, the reader may sometimes feel a slight chill of disappointment. After all, Skelton had been storing up his gunpowder for years, waiting until the time should come when he might blow folly and depravity to the clouds. But somehow, when the time comes, there is no explosion. It appears that Skelton, like the Chinese, has turned his powder into fireworks.

Speke Parrot,[1] which is the earliest of the poems, is also the most obscure. It seems likely that it was composed piece by piece and distributed in this way among the well-disposed. Some verses indeed, addressed to 'my propire Besse,' seem to have crept into the work by mistake—unless Besse is really Henry VIII in disguise.

It has been suggested that some at least of the obscurity may be due to modern ignorance, but it may also be noted that the scheme of *Speke Parrot* demands a certain amount of incoherence if it is to be completely successful. For Skelton's object is to reproduce the talk of a parrot, which is at times coherent enough, but is also likely to lapse into incomprehensible gibberish. And he is certainly successful: the poem is full of passages such as the following:

Aram was fyred with Caldies fyer called Ur;
Iobab was brought vp in the lande of Hus;

[1] Dyce, II, pp. 1–25.

THE SATIRES

The lynage of Lot toke supporte of Assur;
   Iereboseth is Ebrue, who lyst the cause dyscus.
   Peace, Parrot, ye prate, as ye were *ebrius*:
Howst thé, *lyuer god van hemrik, ic seg*;
In Popering grew peres, whan Parrot was an eg.

What is this to purpose? Ouer in a whynnymeg!
   Hop Lobyn of Lowdeon wald haue e byt of bred;
The iebet of Baldock was made for Jack Leg;
   An arrow vnfethered and without an hed,
   A bagpype without blowynge standeth in no sted:
Some run to far before, some run to far behynde,
Some be to churlysshe, and some be to kynde.

Ic dien serueth for the erstrych fether,
   Ic dien is the language of the land of Beme;
In Affryc tongue *byrsa* is a thonge of lether;
   In Palestina there is Ierusalem.
   Colostrum now for Parot, whyte bred and swete creme!
Our Thomasen she doth trip, our Ienet she doth shayle:
Parrot hath a blacke beard and a fayre grene tayle.
ll. 66–86.

It is easy to see the intention behind such writing as
this. Unpalatable comments may be worked in under
cover of a mass of apparently meaningless verbiage, and
any unfavourable comments can be referred to the parrot.
For all that, as Skelton knew very well, the figure of
Wolsey stands out plain for all to see: the parrot is
astonishingly lucid at times:

He tryhumfythe, he trumpythe, he turnythe all vp and
   downe,
   With, skyregalyard, prowde palyard, vaunteperler, ye
     prate!
Hys woluys hede, wanne, bloo as lede, gapythe over the
   crowne:
   Hyt ys to fere leste he wolde were the garland on hys pate,
   Peregall with all prynces farre passyng hys estate;
For of ower regente the regiment he hathe, *ex qua vi*,
Patet per versus, quod *ex vi bolte harvi*.
ll. 426–432.

JOHN SKELTON

The Cardinal appears in various disguises, as Sadok and Og, Sydrake and Moloc, and under cover of these names he is attacked fiercely and unsparingly. It may be well to point out here that no true criticism of Wolsey is to be expected from Skelton at any time. Nothing whatever is heard of his great abilities, his statesmanship and care for learning, his energy and courage. That he had faults no one can deny, and so far Skelton is speaking the truth. Some of his shafts indeed continue to draw blood, but in the main his picture is a gross caricature and bears very little real relation to its subject. It is like some grotesque and savage cartoon by Gillray or Rowlandson. But it undoubtedly represents the opinion of the majority.[1] They were too near Wolsey to see him as he was, and then, as now, the public was eager first and foremost for news of personal failings. Glimpses of extravagant expenditure, descriptions of palaces, fine clothes and immorality—these were the things which were most eagerly desired, and these are the things which Skelton provides. He is so blinded either by indignation or jealousy that he cannot or will not view the situation even remotely in something of its right perspective.

The staple of his criticism is practically the same in all the satires. Wolsey is denounced for his arrogance and overbearing nature:

> With porpose and graundepose he may fede hym fatte,
>> Thowghe he pampyr not hys paunche with the grete seall:
> We haue longyd and lokyd long tyme for that,
>> Whyche cawsythe pore suters haue many a hongry mele:
>> As presydent and regente he rulythe every deall.

---

[1] See *Rede me and be nott wrothe*, ed. E. Arber, (*English Reprints*), 1871, for several striking parallels with *Colyn Cloute* and *Why come ye nat to Courte?*, especially pp. 20, 26, 29, 55 (where Wolsey's appearance in Hell corresponds almost exactly with the description in *Why come ye nat to Courte?*, ll, 966–91), 57, 60, 106, 113.

See also *A Supplicacyon for the Beggers* c. 1592, ed. Furnivall, E.E.T.S. 1871, pp. 1–8, 11, 14; *A Supplycacioun to oure moste Soueraigne Lorde Kynge Henry the Eyght*, ed. J. M. Cooper, E.E.T.S. 1871, p. 29; A. F. Pollard, *Wolsey*, 1929, pp. 53, 71, 97, 101, 103, 249, 305–314.

THE SATIRES

Now pas furthe, good Parott, ower Lorde be your stede,
In this your journey to prospere and spede!

ll. 309–315.

He desires to gather all into his own hand:

Prepayre yow, Parrot, breuely your passage to take,
  Of Mercury vndyr the trynall aspecte,
And sadlye salute ower solen syre Sydrake,
  And shewe hym that all the world dothe coniecte,
  How the maters he mellis in com to small effecte;
For he wantythe of hys wyttes that all wold rule alone;
Hyt is no lytyll bordon to bere a grete mylle stone:

To bryng all the see into a cheryston pytte,
  To nombyr all the sterrys in the fyrmament,
To rule ix realmes by one mannes wytte,
  To suche thynges ympossybyll reason cannot consente:
  Muche money, men sey, there madly he hathe spente:
Parrot, ye may prate thys vndyr protestacion,
Was neuyr suche a senatour syn Crystes incarnacion.

ll. 323–337.

His supposed low birth is a standing offence to Skelton;
again and again the same taunt appears:

So braynles caluys hedes, so many shepis taylys;
  So bolde a braggyng bocher, and flesshe sold so dere;
So many plucte partryches, and so fatte quaylles;
  So mangye a mastyfe curre, the grete grey houndes pere;
  So bygge a bulke of brow auntlers cabagyd that yere;
So many swannes dede, and so small revell;—
Syns Dewcalyons flodde, I trow, no man can tell.

ll. 477–483.

But this is not all: he is extravagant and wasteful, glut-
tonous, impious and unjust, a lecher, loathesomely
diseased. Every evil condition known to the mind of man
is heaped upon his head. Skelton had abused Sir Richard
Garnesche years before in very much the same manner,
but this is much more than a mere accumulation of epithets. Genuine hatred burns in every line: the poet's
words come from his pen white hot.

103

JOHN SKELTON

He is not entirely preoccupied with Wolsey, however, and it is possible to disentangle his views on the state of a society in which such a man can live and wax great. These are in essence simple. The Church is chiefly to blame for the situation. She has neglected her sacred duties, and the resulting chaos is largely of her making. Let her put her house in order and all will be well. She must not interfere in non-ecclesiastical affairs: Skelton, a consistently loyal subject of Henry VIII, is very firm on this point. Church and State must work quietly together in harmony and maintain the true balance of affairs, now upset by purposeless and unprofitable antagonism.

In *Colyn Cloute*[1] these criticisms are expanded, developed, and presented with clarity and force. Skelton now appears simply as a friend of the people. He is their spokesman, and he knows what they want: he is the man in the street, who hears what is reported in the shops and taverns:

> Thus I, Colyn Cloute,
> As I go aboute,
> And wandrynge as I walke,
> I here the people talke.

ll. 287–290.

His intention is to report and comment upon what he hears, plainly and without malicious intent: no one can object to what he says, for his rebukes are not directed at honest men:

> Of no good bysshop speke I,
> Nor good preest I escrye,
> Good frere, nor good chanon,
> Good nonne, nor good canon,
> Good monke, nor good clercke,
> Nor yette of no good werke:
> But my recountyng is
> Of them that do amys,
> In speking and rebellyng,

---

[1] Dyce, I, pp. 34–60.

THE SATIRES

In hynderyng and dysauaylyng
Holy Churche, our mother,
One agaynst another;
To vse suche despytyng
Is all my hole wrytyng;
To hynder no man,
As nere as I can,
For no man haue I named:
Wherfore sholde I be blamed?
Ye ought to be ashamed,
Agaynst me to be gramed,
And can tell no cause why,
But that I wryte trewly.

ll. 1097–1118.

'It would be difficult,' says Professor Berdan, 'to conceive a framework at once more flexible and more irritating than this. He is the friend who brings you unpleasant rumours about yourself . . . because he feels that you should know what is being said . . . one cannot argue—he does not say that he believes what he says—nor can you object to him—he tells you with the kindest of motives. You gnash your teeth in silent fury while he exhorts you to patience.'[1] This loose flexible framework is moreover ideal for the rapid survey which Skelton intends to make. *Why come ye nat to Courte?* is concerned almost exclusively with the personal defects of Wolsey and their effect on conditions within the realm. In *Colyn Cloute* the emphasis lies equally on broader considerations: the situation is described more soberly and with a relatively greater sense of proportion.

Skelton begins by offering an apology for the undignified verse in which he proposes to write, and no-one has described one aspect of his favourite metre with more exactness:

For though my ryme be ragged,
Tattered and iagged,

[1] *Op. cit.*, p. 180.

> Rudely rayne beaten,
> Rusty and moughte eaten,
> If ye take well therwith,
> It hath in it some pyth.   ll. 53–58.

He is right. Pith there is, in great plenty, and his opinions
are stated clearly and forcibly from the start:

> It is wronge with eche degre:
> For the temporalte
> Accuseth the spiritualte;
> The spirituall agayne
> Dothe grudge and complayne
> Vpon the temporall men:
> Thus eche of other blother
> The tone agayng the tother:
> Alas, they make me shoder!
> For in hoder moder
> The Churche is put in faute;
> The prelates ben so haut,
> They say, and loke so hy,
> As though they wolde fly
> Aboue the sterry skye.   ll. 60–74.

Here Skelton and Erasmus are agreed. The Church has
set a bad example: proud and arrogant prelates have forgotten the obligations of their sacred office: they live in
luxury and idleness while the poor starve at their doors.
The humbler clergy also are unworthy servants: they are
not selected with due care, and ignorance is rife within
their ranks:

> In you the faute is supposed,
> For that they are not apposed
> By iust examinacyon
> In connyng and conuersacyon;
> They haue none instructyon
> To make a true constructyon:
> A preest without a letter,
> Without his vertue be gretter,
> Doubtless were moche better
> Vpon hym for to take

A mattocke or a rake.
Also, for very shame!
Some can not declyne their name;
Some can not scarsly rede,
And yet he wyll not drede
For to kepe a cure,
And in nothyng is sure;
This *Dominus vobiscum*,
As wyse as Tom a thrum,
A chaplayne of trust
Layth all in the dust.

ll. 266–286.

Small wonder is it that the lay folk are as a sheep lacking a
shepherd. They are becoming demoralized and worse:
despairing of help from those who should be their spiri-
tual guides they are tempted into the pursuit of heretical
doctrines:

And some haue a smacke
Of Luthers sacke,
And a brennyng sparke
Of Luthers warke,
And are somewhat suspecte
In Luthers secte;
And some of them barke,
Clatter and carpe
Of that heresy arte
Called Wicleuista,
The deuelysshe dogmatista;
And some be Hussyans,
And some be Arryans,
And some be Pollegians,
And make moche varyans
Bytwene the clergye
And the temporaltye,
Howe the Church hath to mykel,
And they haue to lytell, . . .

ll. 542–560.

If the bishops would but attend to their duty reformation
would speedily follow, and the sights which daily distress

the pious, the spectacle of monks and nuns wandering abroad in the world, heresy rearing up its head, ignorant clergy in the pulpit, mercenary friars imposing on ignorant folk and robbing the parish priest of his dues, would soon be things of the past.

Unfortunately the arrogance, and indeed the ignorance, of the bishops is so great that they will countenance no suspicion of criticism:

> With them the worde of God
> Is counted for no rod;
> They counte it for a raylyng,
> That nothyng is auaylyng;
> The prechers with euyll hayling:
> Shall they daunt vs prelates,
> That be theyr prymates?
> Not so hardy on theyr pates!
> Herke, howe the losell prates,
> With a wyde wesaunt!
> Auaunt, syr Guy of Gaunt!
> Auaunt, lewde preest, auaunt!
> Auaunt, syr doctour Deuyas!
> Prate of thy matyns and thy masse,
> And let our maters passe:
> Howe darest thou, daucocke, mell?
> Howe darest thou, losell,
> Allygate the gospell
> Agaynst vs of the counsell?
> Auaunt to the deuyll of hell!
> Take hym, wardeyne of the Flete,
> Set hym fast by the fete!
> I say, lyeutenaunt of the Toure,
> Make this lurdeyne for to loure;
> Lodge hym in Lytell Ease,
> Fede hym with beanes and pease!　ll. 1147–1172.

It is of course Wolsey who is chiefly to blame for this distressing situation: compared with him all the other offenders are as nothing. His leaven has leavened the whole lump, and it is obviously futile to blame too

THE SATIRES

harshly the smaller fry who follow his lead: they are
rather to be pitied and despised. The familiar taunts are
cast at him, but here they are much more detailed and
elaborate than those of *Speke Parrot*. Skelton is not content with mere statements: he gives chapter and verse, or
something like it, for his assertions:

> And where the prelates be
> Come of lowe degre,
> And set in maieste
> And spirituall dyngnyte,
> Farwell benygnyte,
> Farwell symplicite,
> Farwell humylyte,
> Farwell good charyte!
>   Ye are so puffed wyth pryde,
> That no man may abyde
> Your hygh and lordely lokes:
> Ye cast vp then your bokes,
> And vertue is forgotten;
> For then ye wyll be wroken
> Of euery lyght quarell,
> And call a lorde a iauell,
> A knyght a knaue ye make;
> Ye bost, ye face, ye crake,
> And vpon you ye take
> To rule bothe kynge and kayser;
> And yf ye may haue layser,
> Ye wyll brynge all to nought,
> And that is all your thought: . . .

> ll. 587–609.

The circumstances of Wolsey's low birth and upbringing
are recounted at some length:

> Brought vp of poore estate,
> Wyth pryde inordinate,
> Sodaynly vpstarte
> From the donge carte,
> The mattocke and the shule,
> To reygne and to rule:

And haue no grace to thynke
Howe ye were wonte to drynke
Of a lether bottell
With a knauysshe stoppell,
Whan mamockes was your meate,
With moldy brede to eate;
Ye cowde none other gete
To chewe and to gnawe,
To fyll therwith your mawe;
Loggyng in fayre strawe,
Couchyng your drousy heddes
Somtyme in lousy beddes.
Alas, this is out of mynde!
Ye growe nowe out of kynde:
Many one ye haue vntwynde,
And made the commons blynde.

ll. 644-665.

His extravagant expenditure is illustrated by a description
of his great palace at Hampton Court:

Buyldyng royally
Theyr mancyons curyously,
With turrettes and with toures,
With halles and with boures,
Stretchynge to the starres,
With glasse wyndowes and barres;
Hangynge aboute the walles
Clothes of golde and palles,
Arras of ryche aray,
Fresshe as flours in May;
Wyth dame Dyana naked;
Howe lusty Venus quaked,
And howe Cupyde shaked
His darte, and bent his bowe
For to shote a crowe
At her tyrly tyrlowe;
And howe Parys of Troy
Daunced a lege de moy,
Made lusty sporte and ioy
With dame Helyn the quene;

110

With suche storyes bydene
Their chambres well besene
With triumphes of Cesar,
And of Pompeyus war,
Of renowne and of fame
By them to get a name:
Nowe all the worlde stares,
How they ryde in goodly chares,
Conueyed by olyphantes,
With lauryat garlantes,
And by vnycornes
With their semely hornes;
Vpon these beestes rydynge,
Nakes boyes strydynge,
With wanton wenches winkyng.
Nowe truly, to my thynkynge,
That is a speculacyon
And a mete meditacyon
For prelates of estate,
Their courage to abate
From worldly wantonnesse, . . . [1]   ll. 936–976.

Skelton's fears that Wolsey will eventually rule the King and become all-powerful in the kingdom are again expressed with great vigour:

For the communalte dothe reporte
That they haue great wonder
That ye kepe them so vnder;
Yet they meruayle so moche lesse,
For ye play so at the chesse,
As they suppose and gesse,
That some of you but late
Hath played so checkemate
With lordes of great estate,
After suche a rate,
That they shall mell nor make,
Nor vpon them take,
For kynge nor kayser sake,

[1] See Berdan, *op. cit.*, pp. 196–99.

III

But at the playsure of one
That ruleth the roste alone.

ll. 1007–1021.

It is noticeable, however, that though the import of these remarks is perfectly clear, Skelton does not always state positively that it is Wolsey to whom they refer. He attacks him under cover of a diatribe against prelates in general. It is the bishops, the 'Ydolles of Babylon', who

Loue to go trym
Brought up of poore estate.

It is prelates in general, one is asked to believe, who waste other people's substance

Buyldyng royally
Theyr mancyons curyously;

but the veil has worn very thin by this time, and these half-hearted evasions deceive nobody, as Skelton must have known very well.

Colyn Cloute is Skelton at his best, handling his ragged rhyme with consummate skill and virtually inexhaustible in image and phrase. The poem moves with amazing speed, and though it contains over twelve hundred lines it seems almost brief in the reading. The thought is closely packed, and though Skelton is occasionally led astray by his old fondness for stringing together as many rhymes as possible he seldom worries an idea to death. The whole situation is viewed with considerable clarity and brought home to the reader with a conviction and force such as he had never exhibited before. The delicacy of *Phyllyp Sparowe* has almost disappeared: the verse of *Colyn Cloute* is wholly masculine, disdaining ornament and employed exclusively in the presentation of fact. English to the core, it is full of allusions to the common folk of England, Jill and 'Jack of the Noke,' and to traditional comic matter, 'Robyn Swyne,' for example, and that delightful animal, 'Waltom's calfe,' which ran, it may be remembered, nine miles to suck a bull. Margery and Maude and Petronylla look out of the page for a moment and then vanish away like something seen from the window of an express train. Every line of the poem is alive with vitality: by its side aureate verse and fine conceits shrink and crumble into nothing. Skelton is at work on a subject which he knows how to handle as a smith knows how to shoe a horse: indeed his points are driven in like nails. The accumulated thoughts and opinions of half a lifetime are out at last, and they rush from Skelton's mind like children out of school.

The same virility and speed appear in *Why come ye nat to Courte?*[1] also, but the impression which this poem makes is very different. Skelton is almost hysterical in his anger: his voice rises to a scream. Some attempt is made to review the state of affairs within the nation: topical allusions are numerous and clearer than usual, but there is little trace of the balance and proportion which are exhibited by *Colyn Cloute*. Wolsey is now more than a mere tyrant: he is a warlock, an unclean thing, a devil from the nethermost pit:

> He ruleth all the roste
> With braggynge and with bost;
> Borne vp on euery syde
> With pompe and with pryde,
> With, trompe vp, alleluya!
> For dame Philargerya
> Hathe so his herte in holde,
> He loueth nothyng but golde;
> And Asmodeus of hell
> Maketh his membres swell
> With Dalyda to mell,
> That wanton damosell.
> Adew, Philosophia,
> Adew, Theologia!
> Welcome, dame Simonia,
> With dame Castrimergia,
> To drynke and for to eate

[1] Dyce, II, pp. 26–67.

JOHN SKELTON

Swete ypocras and swete meate!
To kepe his flesshe chast,
In Lent for a repast
He eateth capons stewed,
Fesaunt and partriche mewed,
Hennes, checkynges, and pygges;
He foynes and he frygges,
Spareth neither mayde ne wyfe:
This is a postels lyfe!

ll. 198–223.

Skelton's sense of humour has so far deserted him that he even suggests that Wolsey's power over the King has been obtained by the exercise of magic arts:

But what his grace doth thinke,
I haue no pen nor inke
That therwith can mell;
But wele I can tell
How Frauncis Petrarke,
That moche noble clerke,
Wryteth how Charlemayn
Coude nat him selfe refrayne,
But was rauysht with a rage
Of a lyke dotage:
But how that came aboute,
Rede ye the story oute,
And ye shall fynde surely
It was by nycromansy,
By carectes and coniuracyon,
Vnder a certeyne constellacion,
And a xerteyne fumygacion,
Vnder a stone on a golde ryng,
Wrought to Charlemayn the king,
Whiche constrayned him forcebly
For to loue a certayne body
Aboue all other inordinatly.
This is no fable nor no lye;
At Acon it was brought to pas,
As by myne auctor tried it was.
But let mi masters mathematical

THE SATIRES

Tell you the rest, for me they shal;
They haue the full intellygence,
And dare vse the experyens,
In there obsolute consciens
To practyue suche abolete sciens;
For I abhore to smatter
Of one so deuyllysshe a matter.

ll. 680–712.

The stock criticisms and warnings appear, but they have
a more than usually unpleasant air about them:

But I wyll make further relacion
Of this isagogicall colation,
How maister Gaguine, the crownycler
Of the feytis of war
That were done in Fraunce,
Maketh remembraunce,
How Kynge Lewes of late
Made vp a great astate
Of a poore wretchid man,
Wherof moche care began.
Iohannes Balua was his name,
Myne auctor writeth the same;
Promoted was he
To a cardynalles dygnyte
By Lewes the kyng aforesayd,
With hym so wele apayd,
That he made him his chauncelar
To make all or to mar
And to rule as him lyst,
Tyll he cheked at the fyst,
And agayne all reason
Commyted open trayson
And against his lorde souerayn;
Wherfore he suffred payn,
Was hedyd, drawen, and quarterd,
And dyed stynkingly marterd.

ll. 712–738.

The final gibe which Skelton flings at Wolsey is perhaps
the most savage thing he ever wrote:

115

JOHN SKELTON

This Naman Sirus,
So fell and so irous,
So full of malencoly,
With a flap afore his eye,
Men wene that he is pocky,
Or els his surgions they lye,
For, as far as they can spy
By the craft of surgery,
It is *manus Domini*,
And yet this proude Antiochus,
He is so ambicious,
So elate, and so vicious,
And so cruell hertyd,
That he wyll nat be conuertyd;
For he setteth God apart,
He is nowe so ouerthwart,
And so payned with pangis,
That all his trust hangis
In Balthasor, whiche heled
Domingos nose that was wheled;
That Lumberdes nose meane I,
That standeth yet awrye;
It was nat heled alderbest,
It standeth somwhat on the west;
I meane Domyngo Lomelyn,
That was wont to wyn
Moche money of the kynge
At the cardys and haserdynge:
Balthasor, that helyd Domingos nose
From the puskylde pocky pose,
Now with his gummys of Araby
Hath promised to hele our cardinals eye;
Yet sum surgions put a dout,
Lest he wyll put it clene out,
And make him lame of his neder limmes:
God sende him sorowe for his sinnes!

ll. 1163–1198.

Enough has been quoted to show that *Why come ye nat to Courte?* contributes little or nothing that is new either to

Skelton's reputation or to the value of his criticism, though the poem possesses many real merits. Vivid phrases abound: the power and effectiveness of much of the writing are almost beyond praise. But as a whole the poem is disjointed and incoherent. It is *Agaynst Garnesche* over again: Skelton often seems to be gasping for breath.

But there is no attempt at subterfuge: at last the poet and the Cardinal stand face to face. It is just possible that *Colyn Cloute*, or such parts of it as Wolsey saw, was noted, and, for the time being, ignored. But *Why come ye nat to Courte?* must have compelled him to take some definite action. When Skelton first heard that the officers were out is not known: it may well have been somewhere about 1523. During the years of his imprisonment—it was no less—he still continued to write against Wolsey; possibly he added something to the satires already written. By 1529, when he died, Wolsey's power had greatly diminished. It is sad to think that Skelton could not know on his deathbed that his old enemy had himself but a few months to live.

II

SKELTON AND SCOTLAND

Skelton's hatred of the Scots seems to have been almost a constitutional matter. The greater part of it may possibly be due to his early life in the North, where the Scots and their villainies loomed very large on the horizon. It is at any rate a fact that he never loses a chance of an opprobrious epithet or a slighting reference whenever it can be legitimately used. In *Why come ye nat to Courte?* the Scots

> . . . play their olde pranckes;
> After Huntleybankes,

and at all times of his life Skelton seems to have regarded these pranks as an intolerable affliction. He had already, before Flodden, declared his scorn of Dundas (*Vilitissimus Scotus Dundas alleget caudos contra Angligenas*[1]) and others like him. Master John Skelton with a tail? He had writhed under the imputation, and from a member of the hated race to boot:

> Dundas,
> That dronke asse,
> That ratis and rankis,
> That prates and prankes
> On Huntley bankes,
> Take this our thankes;
> Dunde, Dunbar,
> Walke, Scot,
> Walke, sot,
> Rayle not to far.   ll. 54–63.

This poem is largely an academic matter, but no enthusiasm needed to be worked up over the subject of Flodden Field. The existence of the tails of Englishmen was at least problematical: a complete discomfiture of the Scottish forces, with Henry VIII away in France, was a positive and delightful fact, and Skelton was not slow to take full advantage of it.

Against the Scottes[2] is a typically vigorous piece of work, and excellent abuse in its way, but the tone of it is, to say the least, unfortunate. Skelton's indiscriminate and ungenerous whoops against James I, who died fighting on the battlefield, offend very quickly, though one is compelled, as usual, to admire the vivid quality of the writing. That such apology for the author is not a modern innovation appears from the epilogue, written under protest 'Vnto Diuers People That Remord This Rymynge

---

[1] Dyce, I, pp. 192–4.
[2] Dyce, I, pp. 182–9. There was an earlier and shorter version of this poem, *A Ballade of the Scottysshe Kynge*, ed. J. Ashton, 1882 (a facsimile of the original edition). Brie, *loc. cit.*, prints the two versions side by side and gives a full account of the differences between them.

Agaynst the Scot Jemmy.' Critics of such a worthy performance, Skelton thinks, are traitors, and lack discernment. James was certainly the brother,

> Brother vnnatural
> Vnto our kynge royall . . . .

but

> He was a recrayed knyght,
> A subtyll sysmatyke,
> Ryght nere an heretyke,
> Of grace out of the state,
> And died excomunycate.

There can be little respect for Henry in those who object to just criticism of such a fellow: hollow-hearted they are, and no true subjects. '*Si veritatem dico*', he asks ingenuously, '*quare non creditis mihi?*'

The poem concerns itself with all the negotiations of the campaign, the challenge delivered to Henry, away at Terouenne, the advance to Norham Castle, and the details of the battle. A compliment is naturally introduced to the Earl of Surrey:

> The Whyte Lyon, there rampaunt of moode,
> He ragyd and rent out your hart bloode;
> He the Whyte, and ye the Red,
> The Whyte three slew the Red starke ded.
> Thus for your guerdon quyt ar ye,
> Thanked be God in Trinite,
> And swete Sainct George, our ladies knyght!
> Your eye is out; adew, good nyght!
>
> ll. 135–142.

Other similar allusions lend colour to the narrative. Reference is made to the Seven Sisters, the famous cannon from Edinburgh Castle, and the rough and uncouth appearance of the Scots forms the subject of amused comment. At times however a very real and fervent patriotism makes itself felt:

> At Floddon hyllys
> Our bowys, our byllys,

JOHN SKELTON

> Slewe all the floure
> Of theyr honoure.

ll. 25–28.

This is Drayton's Agincourt: the note, though harsher, is the same.

Skelton's love of England is very real, though his enthusiasm occasionally overreaches itself. It can be seen throughout the satires, though it is sometimes drowned in the rush and tumult of mere epithet. The welfare of the land is at the root of much of his criticism, and his reverence for the King is a compound of both patriotic and personal elements. The failure of Henry to quiet the growing disorder is regarded by Skelton from what seems at times to be an almost self-accusatory point of view. His violence against the Scots becomes intelligible on these grounds alone, when it is remembered that here for once is a genuine victory, with no attendant disadvantageous circumstances.

Howe the Douty Duke of Albany[1] is a much later composition on the same theme, and is concerned with the frustrated attempt of the Regent (during James V's minority) to invade the Border in 1523. The procedure is the same, and the tone of the satire is made even more gleeful by the additional diversion afforded by the presence of the French:

> Ge heme, ranke Scot, ge heme,
> With fonde Fraunces, French kyng:
> Our mayster shall you brynge
> I trust, to lowe estate,
> And mate you with chekmate.   ll. 382–386.

Skelton's praises of Henry are now almost incoherent: the King is compared with Hercules, Solomon, and Absalom, Hector, Ptolemy, 'Duke Iosue,' and 'the valiaunt Machube.' In the end he modestly confesses that the task is too great for him: Henry's virtues are so numerous that his

[1] Dyce, II, pp. 68–84.

lernyng is to small
For to recount them all;

but still he perseveres, and begins again with a description of Henry's care for the good of the realm, the
benignity and kindness of his rule. That the impertinent
and graceless Scots should dare to criticize so exemplary a
prince stamps them at once as rascals.

Albany on the other hand receives treatment uncom-
monly similar to that meted out to Sir Christopher Garnesche. No epithet is too low, no image too repulsive,
to characterize such a coward and 'false rebell.' Even the
familiar mock titles are heaped prodigally upon him:

Syr duke, nay, syr ducke,
Syr drake of the lake, sir ducke
Of the donghyll . . .
But hyde thé, sir Topias,
Nowe into the castell of Bas,
And lurke there, lyke an as,
With some Scotyshe (l)as,
With dugges, dugges, dugges:
I shrewe thy Scottishe lugges,
Thy munpynnys, and thy crag,
For thou can not but brag,
Lyke a Scottyshe hag:
Adue nowe, sir Wrig wrag,
Adue, sir Dalyrag!

ll. 222–4 ; 287–297.

Skelton has little but indiscriminate abuse to offer, and
even the patriotic note, the most pleasing feature of the
poem, is forced and unreal. One is faced with the uncom-
fortable suspicion that the author is writing for effect,
attempting to convince enemies of his own loyalty, to
protect himself against accusations which he will not be,
in his heart, surprised to hear. It is difficult to account
otherwise for his apparent reverence for

. . . the noble powre
Of my lorde cardynall,
As an hoost royall,

121

JOHN SKELTON

After the auncient manner,
With sainct Cutberdes banner,
And sainct Williams also;

ll. 59–64.

unless, for once, Skelton is prepared to identify even Wolsey with the interest of England.

Howe the Douty Duke of Albany is very much inferior to *Against the Scottes* in language and in point, but neither poem is distinguished, and both show to an even greater extent than do the Wolsey poems the fatal defects of Skelton's satirical equipment. From beginning to end he exhibits not the slightest attempt at selection or balance of judgment. There is no compression and no subtlety: none of those caustic and sudden phrases which brighten the pages of Swift—and indeed the pages of *Colyn Cloute* —like a flash of lightning: above all nothing of that subtle and devastating irony without which no satire can hope to be completely successful. The monotony of the general tone is infuriating: the ear wearies of the ceaseless rattle of gross and often pointless verbiage. At the end the mind is confused and enervated. One begins to wonder if, after all, there is not a good deal to be said for the wretched Scots. The reaction is inevitable, and it is a result that Skelton never considered even for a moment. With even a little more sensitiveness he might have been at least the second of English satirists. No one ever squandered language more fruitlessly: few have possessed his extraordinary range of expression. His constant and unconscious vitiation of his own powers is one of the real tragedies of literature.

CHAPTER IX

A POET'S FAITH

I

'THE GARLANDE OF LAURELL'

IT is pleasant to come upon an oasis in this desert of scorn and suspicion, to find that Skelton has after all lost nothing of his old love for the leisured and graceful poetry of his youth. To pass from the satires to *The Garlande of Laurell*[1] is to come from a rowdy political meeting, aflame with hatred and acrimony, into a quiet garden filled with the grace and dignity of centuries.

Somewhere about 1523 Skelton journeyed up north to Yorkshire, as the guest of the Countess of Surrey at her castle of Sheriffhutton. The Countess, who was the second wife of that Thomas Howard who became Duke of Norfolk on the death of his father in 1524, was Skelton's friend and patroness, though no more is known of the matter than what *The Garlande of Laurell* itself relates. The impression however which is obtained from the sparsely scattered references is uniformly pleasant, a glimpse of genuine friendliness and appreciation. Skelton appears in a new light, no longer the rude railing rhymster, the scourge of Wolsey, the haunter of taverns, but once again the scholar, the polished wit, the man who had caused William Caxton to remove his cap in admiration over thirty years before. The Countess's son, Henry Howard, was seven years old at this time, and it is tempting to wonder what he thought of his mother's old and distinguished guest. He was to do great things later, and help to usher in the greatest body of poetry that the

[1] Dyce, I, pp. 361–424. See A. S. Cook, *Mod. Lang. Rev.*, Jan. 1916, for an interesting comparison between *The Garlande of Laurell* and Chaucer's *Hous of Fame*.

world has ever seen, but Skelton by that time was dead and already almost forgotten.

It was now nearly twenty years since the last word of *The Bowge of Courte* had been written, but Skelton returns easily to his old methods. The reader is back again, not in Harwich port, but in the mediaeval garden, where poets dream of things never seen on sea or land. After the din and fury of the satires it is pleasantly soothing to hear again gracious and well-worn phrases:

> Arectyng my syght towarde the zodyake,
>   The sygnes xii for to beholde a farre,
> When Mars retrogradant reuersyd his bak,
>   Lorde of the yere in his orbicular,
>   Put vp his sworde, for he cowde make no warre,
> And whan Lucina plenarly did shyne,
> Scorpione ascendynge degrees twyse nyne;
>
> In place alone then musynge in my thought
>   How all thynge passyth as doth the somer flower,
> On euery halfe my reasons forthe I sought,
>   How oftyn fortune varyeth in an howre,
>   Now clere wether, forthwith a stormy showre;
> All thynge compassyd, no perpetuyte,
> But now in welthe, now in aduersyte.
>
> ll. 1–14.

The poet, musing alone, considering the instability of all things, and growing weary, rests himself against the stump of an oak and at once begins to dream:

> As one in a trans or in an extasy,
> I sawe a pauylyon wondersly disgysede,
>   Garnysshed fresshe after my fantasy,
>   Enhachyde with perle and stones preciously,
> The grounde engrosyd and bet with bourne golde,
> That passynge goodly it was to beholde: . . . .
>
> ll. 37–42.

It is not surprising to learn that no less a person than Dame Pallas herself is within the pavilion, listening to the

complaints of the Queen of Fame that Skelton has lately
grown idle and now hardly deserves a place in her court.
After a lengthy and learned conversation the two god-
desses decide to review all the poets of the world:

> To se if Skelton wyll put hymselfe in prease
> Amonge the thickeste of all the hole rowte; . . . .

Eolus blows a blast on his trumpet, and soon a thousand
poets are assembled together, led by Phoebus himself:

> Of laurell leuis a cronell on his hede,
>   With heris encrisped yalowe as the golde,
> Lamentyng Daphnes, whome with the darte of lede
>   Cupyde hath stryken so that she ne wolde
>   Concente to Phebus to haue his herte in holde,
> But, for to preserue her maidenhode clene,
> Transformyd was she into the laurell grene.
>
> ll. 288–294.

Homer is there and Cicero; Virgil, Terence, Boethius,
Poggio and Petrarch; and lastly, the three great Englishmen, Chaucer, Gower and Lydgate, all dressed in gor-
geous habiliments:

> Togeder in armes, as brethern, enbrasid;
>   There apparell farre passynge beyonde that I can tell;
> With diamauntis and rubis there tabers were trasid,
>   None so ryche stones in Turkey to sell;
>   Thei wantid nothynge but the laurell;
> And of there bounte they made me godely chere,
> In maner and forme as ye shall after here.
>
> ll. 393–399.

They greet Skelton kindly and pay him compliments,
after which they go into the pavilion, where Skelton is
met by 'Occupacyon, Famys regestary,' who takes him
round the grounds and entertains him with her conversation. At last they come upon the Countess of Surrey,
sitting 'honorably' in a chair, surrounded by her maidens
busily working at their embroidery. The work they are
engaged upon is nothing less than a laurel crown for

Skelton, and they make of it a very beautiful thing. They work with great diligence:

> Sume to enbrowder put them in prese,
> Well gydyng ther glowtonn to kepe streit theyr sylk,
> Sum pirlyng of goldde theyr worke to encrese
> With fingers smale, and handis whyte as mylk;
> With, Reche me that skane of tewly sylk;
> And, Wynde me that botowme of such an hew,
> Grene, rede, tawny, whyte, blak, purpill, and blew.
>
> ll. 794–800.

In return for their friendly labour the poet courteously devises a little poem for each of them, and then, placing his laurel crown upon his head, he joins Chaucer and his friends, who are charmed with it, declaring that all others are 'counterfeit' in comparison.

It is now time for Skelton to justify his claim to a place in the court of the Queen of Fame, and this must be determined by a recital of his works. Occupacyon comes forward with her book of remembrance, a sumptuous volume:

> The margent was illumynid all with golden railles
> And byse, enpicturid with gressoppes and waspis,
> With butterflyis and fresshe pecoke taylis,
> Enflorid with flowris and slymy snaylis;
> Enuyuid picturis well towchid and quikly;
> It wolde haue made a man hole that had be ryght sekely,
>
> To beholde how it was garnysshed and bounde,
> Encouerde ouer with golde of tissew fyne;
> The claspis and bullyons were worth a thousande pounde;
> With balassis and charbuncles the borders did shyne;
> With *aurum musicum* euery other lyne
> Was wrytin: and so she did her spede,
> Occupacyoun, inmediatly to rede.
>
> ll. 1157–1169.

The list which Occupacyon reads is, we are informed, incomplete, 'in as moche as it were to longe a proces to reherse all by name that he hath compylyd,' but the verdict is of course a foregone conclusion: the whole assembly at once joins in his praise:

> *Triumpha, triumpha!* they cryid all aboute;
> Of trumpettis and clariouns the noyse went to Rome;
>   The starry heuyn, me thought, shoke with the showte;
>   The grownde gronid and tremblid, the noyse was so
>   stowte:
> The Quene of Fame commaundid shett fast the boke;
>
> ll. 1506–1510.

and the poet, startled by the noise, suddenly awakes from his dream.

Dyce remarks that this poem is the first instance in English of a poet writing sixteen hundred lines in praise of himself, and *The Garlande of Laurell* is undoubtedly an amazing monument of self-glorification. Hardly for a moment does Skelton cease to sound his own praises, and the self-assurance which breathes through the pages is little short of bewildering. But it is all delightfully done, and not at all offensive: the vaunting moreover is for once not at anyone else's expense. His intense conviction of his own importance is amusing, but though posterity has not thought fit to agree with him it will be long before some parts at least of his poem are completely forgotten. It is indeed chiefly by the lyrics addressed to the Countess's young attendants that he is now remembered by readers of poetry. They are perfect in their kind, models of what such occasional compliments should be in the delicacy of their fancy and their musical ease:

> *To mastres Margery Wentworthe.*
>
> With margerain ientyll,
>   The flowrc of goodlyhede,
> Enbrowdred the mantill
>   Is of your maydenhede.
> Plainly I can not glose;
>   Ye be, as I deuyne,
> The praty primrose,

127

JOHN SKELTON

The goodly columbyne.
With margerain iantill,
   The flowre of goodlyhede,
Enbrawderyd the mantyll
   Is of yowre maydenhede.
Benynge, corteise, and meke,
   With wordes well deuysid;
In you, who list to seke,
   Be vertus well comprysid.
With margerain iantill,
   The flowre of goodlyhede,
Enbrowderid the mantill
   Is of yowr maydenhede.   ll. 906–925.

Here Skelton's facility exhibits himself in its most attractive guise: he displays a sensitiveness of ear and a careful handling of words which make it a matter of eternal regret that he did not think fit to amuse himself more often in this way:

To maystres Margaret Hussey.

Mirry Margaret,
As mydsomer flowre,
Ientill as fawcoun
Or hawke of the towre;
   With solace and gladnes,
Moche mirthe and no madnes,
All good and no badnes,
So ioyously,
So maydenly,
So womanly
Her demenyng
In euery thynge,
Far, far passynge
That I can endyght,
Or suffyce to wryght
Of mirry Margarete,
As mydsomer flowre,
Ientyll as fawcoun
Or hawke of the towre;

128

A POET'S FAITH

            As pacient and as styll,
            And as full of good wyll,
            As fayre Isaphill;
            Colyaunder,
            Swete pomaunder,
            Good cassaunder;
            Stedfast of thought,
            Wele made, wele wrought;
            Far may be sought,
            Erst that ye can fynde
            So corteise, so kynde
            As mirry Margarete,
            This midsomer flowre,
            Ientyll as fawcoun
            Or hawke of the towre.   ll. 1004–1037.

The whole poem indeed is full of a sense of ease and
enjoyment, saturated in an atmosphere of holiday and
leisure. Skelton is making the most of a temporary respite
from social and political problems in a last manipulation
of the aureate terms which he loved so well:

    With proper captacyons of beneuolence,
        Ornatly pullysshid after your faculte,
    Sith ye must nedis afforce it by pretence
        Of your professyoun vnto vmanyte,
    Commensyng your proces after there degre,
    To iche of them rendryng thankis commendable,
    With sentence fructuous and termes couenable.
                                ll. 815–821.

No harsh sounds from the outside world disturb the
quiet atmosphere of Sheriffhutton. Here is culture and
refinement: the calm enjoyment of the poet's craft.
Imaginative description, classical reminiscences, literary
criticism, humorous references to contemporaries like
Robert Gaguin,

        That frownyd on me full angerly and pale,

(no doubt remembering early controversies), lyrics, the
inevitable conundrum, Latin verses, even a long quota-

tion from *Phyllyp Sparowe*, all follow one another in a pleasant disorder, and the language, if occasionally over-elaborate, is for the most part luxurious and dignified:

> In the middis a coundight, that coryously was cast,
>   With pypes of golde engusshing out stremes;
> Of cristall the clerenes theis waters far past,
>   Enswymmyng with rochis, barbellis, and bremis,
>   Whose skales ensilured again the son beames
> Englisterd, that ioyous it was to beholde.
>
> ll. 658–663.

Skelton presents his readers with what is virtually an epitome of his practice as a poet in the great tradition of his masters, and constructs a poem which can only be compared with the glorious 'cloth of astate' which covered the Queen of Fame in the enchanted garden. *The Garlande of Laurell* is the last great production of its kind: few literary fashions have had a more distinguished end.

II

THE NEW LEARNING

Something has already been said of Skelton's reactions to the New Learning, his enthusiasm for Latin studies and his courageous but unsuccessful attempt to give the new Greeks a fair hearing. As has been seen, he tried to keep an open mind, but the task was too much for him, and he tells us exactly why.

It is the presumption of the new men which he finds so peculiarly irritating: he is appalled at the indecent haste with which they have begun to set the world to rights. The old, careful, scrupulous, and laborious methods of study seem to be already things of the past, and nothing is safe from interference. Even the doctrine of the Church, the sacred province of Theology herself, is subject to callow criticism and impertinent censure:

and yet they were but febly enformed in maister Porphiris
problemes, and haue waded but weakly in his thre maner of
clerkly workes, analeticall, topicall, and logycall: howbeit
they were puffed so full of vaynglorious pompe and surcudant elacyon, that popholy and peuysshe presumpcion
prouoked them to publysshe and to preche to people
imprudent perilously, howe it was idolatry to offre to
ymages of our blessed lady, or to pray and go on pylgrimages,
or to make oblacions to any ymages of sayntes in churches or
els where.[1]

There is something extremely pathetic underlying Skelton's vehemence. Nothing is more clearly indicative of
his fundamental mediaevalism than this futile attempt to
frighten away the spirit of free inquiry by a despairing
appeal to the efficacy of 'maister Porphiris problemes.'
Darkness was beginning to cover the mediaeval world,
though the danger was as yet nothing but a cloud, no
bigger than a man's hand, on the horizon. Skelton is
bewildered and frightened, though he does not care to
admit it even to himself. He looses off his old bolts, fires
off his ancient cannon against the invaders, but somehow
the report does not seem as loud as it used to be, and the
enemy does not check even for a moment in his stride.

Of Skelton's relations with the English Humanists
hardly anything is known, though he must have come
into contact with many of them. Characteristically the
sole record extant concerns a quarrel between the poet

[1] *A Replycacion;* Dyce, I, p. 209. In *The Praise of Folly* Erasmus expresses the
usual Humanistic attitude, though he intensifies and exaggerates it to make his
criticism more effective. See Wilson's translation (1668) ed. Mrs. P. S. Allen,
1925, pp. 115–6. See also R. S. Rait in *Mediaeval England*, Oxford, 1924, pp.
446–7:
'As the sixteenth century advanced there was added to the new love of literature a contempt for the ancient philosophical studies. At one time it appeared as
if this contempt were to involve the universities in the destruction of the monas-
teries, and an Act was introduced into Parliament for the dissolution of the
Colleges.' For a description of mediaeval learning and text-books see *The Auto-
biography of Thomas Platter* (1572), ed. R. Monroe, 1904, p. 12; the *Manuale
Scholarium* (1481) trans. by R. F. Seybolt, 1921, Chapter III; and of course Rashdall, *op. cit.*, particularly Vol. II, p. 456, *et seq.*
I am indebted to Professor G. R. Potter for information on the subject of
mediaeval university education.

and William Lilly the grammarian,[1] the first High Master
of Colet's foundation of St. Paul's School. The indefati-
gable Bale has preserved the initial line of Skelton's poem
against Lilly:

> Urgeor impulsus tibi, Lilli, retundere;

but that is all that is left of his side of the quarrel. Lilly's
reply is extant in full:

> *Lilli Hendecasyllabi in Scheltonum ejus carmina*
> *calumniantem.*
>
> Quid me, Scheltone, fronte sic aperta
> Carpis, vipereo potens veneno?
> Quid versus trutina meos iniqua
> Libras? dicere vera num licebit?
> Doctrinae tibi dum parare famam
> Et doctus fieri studes poeta,
> Doctrinam nec habes, nec es poeta.

It is neatly done, and in some ways a surprisingly just
estimate of one part at least of Skelton's work. Lilly is
speaking what, as he saw it, was the literal truth. Skelton
is neither learned, nor has he the method, nor is he a poet,
as far as the Humanists are concerned. His mediaeval
models are already matter for laughter, 'and since to them
the propriety of writing in English at all was questionable,
the impropriety of writing English based upon such
models was beyond a doubt.'[2] The New Learning, therefore, is in Skelton's view a thing to be profoundly dis-
trusted. It makes inquiries into matters which are best left
undisturbed: it possesses no proper regard for authority
and tradition, and it is breeding a race of thoroughly ob-
jectionable young men, shallow and cocksure, who sneer
at things manifestly venerable, and—this is the last straw
—care not a rap for the opinion of one who has been in
his time one of the most redoubtable scholars in all
England.

Skelton's attempts to convince himself that the great

---

[1] Dyce, I, xxxvii–xxxviii.
[2] See Berdan, *op. cit.*, p. 219.

era of discovery and enlightenment which was now dawning upon Europe was only a passing fashion are pitiable, to say the least, but it is fortunate that he did not live to see more of it. Very quickly what little reputation he had left was taken from him: together with the rest of the mediaeval writers he suffers a sea-change. The dignified scholar and powerful satirist disappears, to re-emerge very soon as a rude clown, a figure of fun, employed in nastiness as befitted one who belonged to a dark and entirely unrefined age. At last he is beastly Skelton: the last leaf drops away from his bedraggled crown.

III

'A REPLYCACION'

Two years before his death, and probably while he was in sanctuary, Skelton wrote his last satire. *A Replycacion Agaynst Certayne Yong Scolars Abiured of Late*[1] was printed by Pynson somewhere about 1528: the pamphlet has no date. The poem could not have been written before 1527, for in that year Thomas Bilney and Thomas Arthur, two Cambridge scholars, abjured their errors before a Council at Westminster, and carried faggots on September 29 in evidence of their repentance, and it was against these men and their detestable opinions that Skelton launched his final broadside.

The circumstances were particularly distressing. In the first place the two scholars were Cambridge men: their University had been put to shame. Skelton, one of the most loyal sons Cambridge has ever had, takes it upon himself to offer her comfort:

Eulogium consolationis.

Alma parens O Cantabrigensis,
Cur lacrymaris? Esto, tui sint

[1] Dyce, I, pp. 206–224.

JOHN SKELTON

Degeneres hi filioli, sed
Non ob inertes, O pia mater,
Insciolos vel decolor esto.
Progenies non nobilis omnis,
Quam tua forsan mamma fovebat.
Tu tamen esto Palladis almae
Gloria pollens plena Minervae,
Dum radiabunt astra polorum:
Jamque valeto, meque foveto,
Namque tibi quondam carus alumnus eram.[1]

It is both a touching and an amusing picture. Let her not weep, for John Skelton is still there. But a 'carus alumnus' he was and had ever been, proud of his University and grateful for kindnesses spread over many years. Now when the time comes he stands up proudly and publishes his pride and gratitude for all to see: faith and loyalty were indeed not the least of his virtues.

It is not only Cambridge however which has been brought to confusion. The two heretics are unfortunately Norfolk men too,[2] men from his own countryside. He feels almost personally responsible and doubly ashamed of their conduct.

The poem however is less a diatribe against the two scholars than a public confession of his own faith, an assertion of his own unshakeable orthodoxy. The worship of the Trinity, the Virgin Mary, and the works of the Saints is proudly defended against all comers, defended by the authority of the Church resident in John Skelton, and by all the great men who have laboured for her welfare in the past. He writes with unmistakable conviction: his poem is no mere attempt to make his peace with authority. This enthusiastic witness for the faith is part and parcel of his similar championship of the old studies, reference to which indeed creeps, with other things, into the poem.[3]

[1] Dyce, I, p. 207.
[2] See J. B. Mullinger, *History of the University of Cambridge*, 1888, I, pp. 563 and note 3; 562, 574.
[3] See also the three prayers or hymns in Dyce, I, pp. 139–40.

A POET'S FAITH

It is an astonishing work for a man of seventy. His vigour is unimpaired, and he varies his material and scatters epithets with an abandon which would have done credit to any earlier period of his life:

> *Sive per aequivocum,*
> *Sive per univocum,*
> *Sive sic, sive* nat so,
> Ye are brought to, Lo, lo, lo!
> Se where the heretykes go,
> Wytlesse wandring to and fro!
> With, Te he, ta ha, bo ho, bo ho!
> And suche wondringes many mo.
>
> Helas, ye wreches, ye may be wo!
> Ye may syng wele away,
> And curse bothe nyght and day,
> Whan ye were bredde and borne,
> And whan ye were preestes shorne,
> Thus to be laughed to skorne,
> Thus tattred and thus torne,
> Thorowe your owne foly,
> To be blowen with the flye
> Of horryble heresy.
> Fayne ye were to reny,
> And mercy for to crye,
> Or be brende by and by,
> Confessyng howe ye dyde lye
> In prechyng shamefully.[1]

ll. 69–91.

The verse runs easily and carries the reader along with it: if it were not for what is known of the circumstances of its composition it would be difficult to know where to place the poem in the canon of Skelton's works.

[1] Compare Sir Thomas More, *Dialogue concerning Tyndale*, ed. W. E. Campbell, 1927, p. 11:
'Vpon these words, and other like, when I considered that your friend was studious of scripture, and although I now have a very good opinion of him . . . yet, to be plain with you and him both, by reason that he hath set the matter so well and lustily forward, he put one somewhat in doubt whether he were, as young scholars be sometimes prone to new fantasies, fallen into Luther's sect.' See also pp. 13, 60, 80, 117, 120, 146–75, 194–5, 244, for an illuminating commentary on much of this poem.

JOHN SKELTON

The content of *A Replycacion* is however not exclusively theological. The most delightful thing in the poem is a noble poetic credo, which does Skelton infinite credit. Towards the end of the work he takes an opportunity of replying to critics who have asserted that there are matters which it is better for poets to leave alone:

> Ye saye that poetry
> Maye nat flye so hye
> In theology,
> Nor analogy,
> Nor philology,
> Nor philosophy,
> To answere or reply
> Agaynst suche heresy.
> Wherfore by and by
> Nowe consequently
> I call to this rekenyng
> Dauyd, that royall kyng,
> Whom Hieronymus,
> That doctour glorious,
> Dothe bothe write and call
> Poete of poetes all,
> And prophete princypall.
> This may nat be remorded,
> For it is wele recorded
> In his pystell *ad Paulinum*,
> *Presbyterum divinum*,
> Where worde for worde ye may
> Rede what Jerome there dothe say.
> ll. 306–328.

David himself was a poet, greater by far than Horace or Catullus, and he dealt with the greatest of all themes:

> Of our Sauyour Christ in his decacorde psautry,
> That at his resurrection he harped out of hell
> Olde patriarkes and prophetes in heuen with him to dwell.
> ll. 340–342.

But the poet does not need the authority of even David

136

for his justification: the gift of poetry is no less a thing
than the gift of God:

> By whose inflammacion
> Of spyrituall instygacion
> And diuyne inspyracion,
> We are kyndled in suche facyon
> With hete of the Holy Gost,
> Which is God of myghtes most,
> That he our penne dothe lede,
> And maketh in vs suche spede,
> That forthwith we must nede
> With penne and ynke procede,
> Somtyme for affection,
> Somtyme for sadde dyrection,
> Somtyme for correction,
> Somtyme vnder protection
> Of pacient sufferance . . .[1]   ll. 379–393.

It would be impossible to go higher: the passage makes
noble reading. But there is nothing surprising in it; the
root of the matter had been in Skelton from the first,
however overlaid it became later with laurels and embroidered gowns, and the passage explains a good deal of
his irascibility and sensitiveness in the face of criticism.
As a man set apart, singled out by his great gift, such
objections must have goaded him sorely. Here he is far
from mere vanity. The passage moreover suggests another consideration. It is impossible for us to know what
he thought of the poetical value of his political satires:
what is certain is that he used what gifts he had for the
public good as he saw it. As has been suggested, however,
the existence of *The Garlande of Laurell* leads one to think
that there he was engaged in what he considered to be his

---

[1] Boccaccio expresses the same view. Poetry is for him 'whatever of weighty
in argument, deep in doctrine and vivid in imagination the man of genius may
produce with conscious art in prose and verse. Poetry is instruction conveyed
through allegory and fiction. Theology itself is a form of poetry; even the Holy
Ghost may be called a poet, inasmuch as he used the vehicle of symbol in the
visions of the prophets—the revelation of St. John.'—*Genealogia Deorum*, quoted
by J. A. Symonds, *The Renaissance in Italy: the Revival of Learning*, 1909, p. 69.

137

true poetic business, and that the satires, with the exception of *Magnyfycence*, were to him creatures of an hour, cast in a popular form to reach a larger audience, propaganda rather than literature. This high sense of the dignity of his calling is easily reconcilable with a realization of an imperative call to duty: it is at least not unlikely that he may at times have deplored that necessity which repeatedly called him from the fullest exercise of his gifts. Let him conclude in his own words:

> Sunt infiniti, sunt innumerique sophistae,
> Sunt infiniti, sunt innumerique logistae,
> Innumeri sunt philosophi, sunt theologique,
> Sunt infiniti doctores, suntque magistri
> Innumeri; sed sunt pauci rarique poetae.

.   .   .   .   .

The foregoing remarks have attempted to suggest that it will not do to dismiss Skelton briefly as a rude railing rhymster, and, by implication at least, to guard against the equally dangerous view which sees in him a tremendous and neglected genius. For he was neither of these: indeed an unprejudiced eye must in honesty often see an intolerable deal of railing with the small pennyworth of wit. Large tracts of aridity try the patience: pleasant things like *Mirry Margaret* appear by contrast greener perhaps than nature. So much upon over-enthusiasm. To speak at greater length of his merits is an easy and pleasant task.

Looking back over the long range of his work, one is bound to admit that he never entered the promised land, though at times he obtained something of a Pisgah-sight of it. His work is full of unmistakable sign-posts: his poetry, filling to overflowing its mediaeval channels, strays here and there into fascinating rivulets which soon peter out among the sands. Skelton never rises far above

tradition, but for all that he had done with it. At last a
poet had arisen who could squeeze out its juice to the
very last drop. That he was content with that is his misfortune and our own, yet it would be ungrateful to wish
him elsewhere, in more fortunate times. He has a solid
achievement of his own to stand upon, and criticism will
dig a pit for itself if it ventures to border on the patron-
izing.

It is unlikely that he will ever become a popular poet,
except in so far as his more obvious successes appear in
anthologies. Dyce, in offering his great edition 'to a
limited class of readers,' made, whether he realized it or
not, a shrewd comment on his author's work. Skelton's
habits of mind are mediaeval; modernity as we know it
he hardly ever saw, and when he did it was to turn away
from it in suspicion, or to hurl a violent and nervous jeer
against that which seemed to touch his faith too nearly.

On the other hand he is no curiosity-shop figure.
There can hardly have been a poet before or since more
in love with life, more sure of his own great part in the
scheme of things. *Homo sum, humani a me nihil alienum
puto* is his constant cry; man and his work, books, learning, poetry, music, all are his concern. It is indeed with
the man Skelton and not with his work that we have
ultimately to reckon, and to add that the two are the same
is no attempt at qualification. This is always the position
when one is constantly thinking that an author might do
better an he would. What for instance has much of the
work of Dr. Johnson to do with the Samuel Johnson of
Boswell? Skelton unfortunately had no Boswell, but his
talk, one supposes, can hardly have been inferior to that
of the great Lexicographer. What is left to us now is the
mere husk of the man.

Strength and virility, rather than delicacy, mark him
out. Leaving Swift, one looks in vain in English for his
like: he agrees with his great successor in almost everything but his colossal genius. Among his own contem-

poraries he is a Triton among minnows: he towers head
and shoulders above them, and at his firm touch most of
them vanish into nothing. He speaks across the ages in a
strong and confident voice, but 'to a limited class of
readers.' What have we to do now with Wolsey's morals,
or with Skelton's fears that his old pupil is rushing head-
long to ruin? Jane and her sparrow, Mirry Margaret, and
Elynour's ale are different matters. Here Skelton busies
himself for a moment with the universal (though he
would probably have been surprised at the suggestion)
and comes into full view. But even as we look he is gone.

APPENDIX I

SKELTON'S TRANSLATION OF DIODORUS SICULUS

Diodorus Siculus of my translacyon
Out of fresshe Latine into owre Englysshe playne,
Recountyng commoditis of many a straunge nacyon;
Who redyth it ones wolde rede it agayne;
Sex volumis engrosid together it doth containe. . . .

The Garlande of Laurell, ll. 1498–1502.

THIS work, of which the only known MS. is in the library of Corpus Christi College, Cambridge,[1] is a translation of Poggio's Latin version of Diodorus Siculus, first printed at Bologna in 1472, and dedicated to Pope Nicholas V. The 'sex volumis' sound formidable, but the MS. is a normal folio of some 250 pages. It has been suggested that at least part of it is a holograph: Dr. M. R. James speaks of 'the first three leaves written by Skelton in a large Gothic hand.' This is on the whole unlikely,[2] but the opinion of so great a paleographer cannot be summarily dismissed. At least two hands seem to have been at work on the MS.

It is strange to see a page of this translation after an hour, say, with *Colyn Cloute*. To find the muscular, vigorous Skelton stumbling along carefully with the majority of the other fifteenth-century prose-writers is more than a little surprising. Somehow one had expected him to write like Swift.

[1] Catalogue of MSS., 357. I am indebted to the Librarian for permission to examine the MS.
[2] See Brie; *loc. cit.*, L. J. Lloyd in *The Review of English Studies, loc. cit.*, and H. L. R. Edwards, *ibid., loc. cit.*

APPENDIX II

SKELTON'S LOST WORKS

SOME of Skelton's works, no longer extant, have already been mentioned. But the full list in *The Garlande of Laurell*, even though it professes only to enumerate 'sum parte of Skeltons bokes and baladis with ditis of plesure,' is a long one, as follows:

The Boke of Honorous Astate
The Boke how men shulde fle synne
Royal Demenaunce (worshyp to wynne)
The Boke to speke well or be styll
Item to lerne you to dye when ye wyll
Of Vertu . . . the souerayne enterlude
The Boke of the Rosiar
Prince Arturis Creacyoun
The False Fayth that now goth, which dayly is renude
Diologgis of Ymagynacyoun
Automedon of Loues Meditacyoun
His commedy, Achademios
Of Tullis Familiars the translacyoun
Good Aduysement
Recule ageinst Gaguyne
Of Soueraynte a noble pamphelet
Of Mannes Lyfe the Peregrynacioun (translated from the
    French)
The Tratyse of Triumphis of the Rede Rose
The Balade of the Mustard Tarte
The Gruntyng and the groynninge of the gronnyng swyne
The Murnynge of the mapely rote
A deuoute Prayer to Moyses hornis
Epitomis of the myller and his ioly make
Wofully arayd
Vexilla Regis
Sacris solemniis
. . . 'my deuisis I made in disporte

142

APPENDIX II

Of the Mayden of Kent callid Counforte
Of Louers testamentis and of there wanton wyllis
And how Iollas louyd goodly Phillis.'

To this list must no doubt be added, on Skelton's own
testimony, other poems about Manerly Margery and
Mistress Anne; and there are somewhat mysterious
references to 'paiauntis that were played in Ioyows Garde'
and to *The Nacyoun of Folys*. This last is certainly not
Brandt's *Narrenschiff*, or Barclay's *Ship of Fools*. Indeed it
may not be the title of a work at all. Take out the capitals
and it becomes a plain statement of fact; i.e., 'He did not
forget the nation of fools.' The poem goes on: 'Item Apollo
that whirllid vp his chare.' This may simply mean that
the poem about Apollo was one (or one of several)
written to pour ridicule on the world of fools.

At any rate, here is a formidable list of works; though
it does not seem as though many of them have survived,
at least under their present titles. Dyce indeed printed[1]
a poem, *A Lawde and Prayse made for our souereigne Lord
the Kyng*, beginning:

> The Rose both White and Rede
> In one Rose now dothe grow; . . . .

with the comment that this is possibly the 'Boke of the
Rosiar.' Possibly it is; it was found among the Records of
the Receipt of the Exchequer, a fact which in itself might
give rise to fascinating speculation. Mr. Philip Henderson[2]
decides in favour of it, and prints it, (pp. 25–26). Mr.
Henderson also prints (pp. 21–24) a poem beginning:

> Now sing we, as we were wont
> *Vexilla regis prodeunt*; . . .

but it is difficult, without further evidence, to agree that this
is the lost *Vexilla Regis*. Both Mr. Henderson (pp. 12–14)
and Mr. Richard Hughes[3] (pp. 7–9) print, in modernized

---

[1] I, ix–xi.
[2] *The Complete Poems of John Skelton*, 1931.
[3] *Poems, by John Skelton*, 1924.

form, a poem (from Fairfax MS. Add. MSS. 5465, fols. 76 and 86, B.M.) beginning:

> Woefully arrayed
> My blood, man
> For thee ran
> It may not be nay'd. . . . .

which seems to me to be thoroughly unlike Skelton's work. No confidence at all can be placed in a poem, *To his Wife* (!) (Hughes, p. 19; Henderson, p. 207):

> Petevelly
> Constrayned am y.

Brie indeed disposed of it effectively in 1907. For a discussion of Brie's attribution to Skelton of a fragment in Trin. Coll. Camb. MS. O. 2. 53, beginning 'Mastres Anne, I am your man' (Henderson, p. 143), see L. J. Lloyd in *The Review of English Studies* July, 1929. Mr. Henderson also prints (pp. 144–150) '*The maner of the world now a dayes*,' but is inclined to agree with Dyce[1] that the poem is not genuine.

[1] I, pp. 148–154 and II, p. 199.

GLOSSARY

A

Abolete: antiquated; abolished.
Allygate: allege.
Amense: amends.
Antethem: antetyme: text.
Apposed: questioned.
Armatyche: aromatic.
Arras: tapestry. Arras in Artois was a great centre for its manufacture.
Arrecte: raise.
Artyke: Arctic.
Auaunsid: advanced.
Auysynge: advising.
Aurum musicum: (i.e., aurum musaicum): mosaic gold.

B

Bale: sorrow, trouble.
Bas: kiss.
Baudy: dirty, foul.
Bet: adj. better: vb. beaten.
Ble: complexion.
Bloo: livid.
Blerde: bleared.
Blother: babble.
Blowboll: drunkard.
Blynkerd: blinking, bleary-eyed.
Botowme: the nucleus on which a ball was wound: a ball of thread.
Boteles: without remedy; hopeless.
Bourne: burnished.
Brace: boast, brag.
Brayde, at a: at a pinch, suddenly.
Brymly: fiercely.
Bullyons: studs, bosses.
Bydene: together.
Byllys: bills; pikes or halberds.
Byse: blue, also perhaps grey.

C

Cabagyd: cut off close behind the horns. Cf. the heraldic 'caboched.'
Cane: Khan.
Cantell: piece, portion.
Captacyons: compliments.
Capyd: capped.
Carectes: characters, perhaps magical inscriptions.

Cassaunder: Cassandra.
Castrimergia: gluttony.
Chase: a piece of dung.
Cheked: attacked, turned against; a hawking term.
Cockes: God's; 'Cock' is a corruption of God.
Colation: comparison.
Coliaunder: *coriandrum sativum*, an aromatic plant.
Colour: ornament of style or diction in rhetoric.
Congruence: fitness.
Coniecte: conjecture.
Conny: sweetheart.
Connyng: learned.
Controllynge: restraining, putting a check upon.
Copyus: wearing a cope.
Corporas: the linen cloth which covers the consecrated elements.
Couenable: fitting, suitable.
Counte: count (as a title).
Craked: bragged, boasted.
Creauncer: tutor, guardian.
Custrell, coystrell: varlet; low fellow.
Cut, to keep: to be on one's best behaviour.

D

Dale, dyne: dark valley.
Daucocke: fool.
Dauysyd: devised.
Deuyse, at my: according to my pleasure.
Dow: pigeon.
Draffe: refuse, rubbish.
Drawttys: draughts.
Dreggys: dregs.
Dronny: drone, snore.
Dryvyll: drudge, low fellow.
Dyscure: discover.

E

Emportured: portrayed.
Endude: digested; a hawking term.
Engrosyd: enriched.
Enhached: inlaid, adorned.
Ennewed, enneude: coloured, tinted.

GLOSSARY

Enprowed: improved.

Ensaymed: cleaned; purged from superfluous fat; a hawking term.

Enuyuid: lively.

Escrye: call out against.

Estryge: ostrich.

F

Falyre: fellow, darling.

Familiars, Tullis: Cicero, Ad Familiares.

Franchyse: freedom, privileged liberty.

Fet: fetched.

Feytis: feats.

Fonde: foolish.

Fonne: fool.

Fonny: foolish; foolishly amorous.

Fraye: fright.

Fret: adorned.

Frete, freat: devour.

Frowardes: difficulties.

Fysnamy: physiognomy; face.

G

Galles, broken: sore spots.

Gambaudis: gambols.

Garde: made.

Gayne: against.

Gery: giddy.

Geyte, feyty bone: makes a good story.

Gle: blink, squint.

Glose: deceive.

Glowtonn: needle, bodkin.

Glent: glowing brightly.

Gramed: angry.

Graundepose: grampus.

Grotes: groats. The groat was a coin worth fourpence.

Gytes: clothes; gowns.

H

Halow: halloo; call.

Halsyd: embraced. To halse is to embrace round the neck.

Haroldis: heralds.

Hastarddis: rash fellows.

Haute: high, haughty.

Hayling, with euyll: with a curse.

Hoder moder: hugger mugger; confusion.

Hofte: head.

Hoked: hooked.

Holly: wholly.

Hyghte, on: on high.

Hyre: higher.

I

Iavell: a low fellow.

Iebet: gibbet.

Iet: strut.

Indifferent: impartial.

Irous: angry.

Isagogicall: introductory.

K

Knokylbonyarde : a contemptible fellow.

Koy, make it: affect haughtiness.

Kynde: nature.

Kyst: cast.

Kyt: cut.

L

Laftynge: thieving.

Large and longe: characters in old music.

Lazars: lepers.

Ledder: leather, leathern.

Lere: complexion.

Let: hinder, stop.

Lewde: ignorant, unlearned; also poor, worthless, i.e. 'lewde lewte.'

Lorell: rogue, villain.

Losyll: scoundrel.

Loure: frown.

Lowse: vb. lose.

Lumbryth: plays clumsily.

Lurden: clown, rascal.

Lust and lykyng: pleasure and delight.

Lyppers: lepers.

Lyste, garded with a: trimmed, faced with.

Lyther: wicked, lazy.

M

Make: mate, wife.

Mamockes: scraps, shreds, leavings.

Marmoll: an inflamed sore, particularly on the leg.

Mapely: maple.

Mellis: mingles.

Moute, moughte: vb. might.

Mullyng: darling.

Munpynnys: mouth-pegs, teeth.

146

GLOSSARY

Murnynge: mourning.
Musse: mouth.
Mutid: dunged.
Mytyng: sweetheart, darling.

N

Neder: nether, lower.
Nobbes: darling.
Noppe: nap (of cloth).
Nyse: foolish.

O

Orbicular: circle.

P

Paiauntis: pageants.
Palles: palls, rich cloths.
Paltoke: a short coat.
Palyarde: lewd person, rascal.
Parcele: part; portion.
Passynge: surpassing.
Patlet: ruff.
Paynty: pretend.
Peregall: equal.
Perkyd: perched.
Peuysshe: peevish.
Philargerya: love of money.
Pirlyng: winding.
Plete, vb.: plead.
Pollynge: plundering.
Popering: Poperinghe, in the neighbourhood of Calais.
Porpose: porpoise.
Pose: rheum in the head.
Pountesse: Pontoise.
Powle hachet: blockhead.
Poynte deuyse: perfectly.
Pranked: set in order.
Prease, will put himself in: will join the throng.
Prest: ready, neat.
Pryckemedenty: an affected person.
Punyete: pungent, strong.
Puskylde: full of pustules.
Pytte, cheryston: cherry-stone pit: an allusion to a game played with cherry-stones.

R

Railles: rails, marginal decorations in straight lines?
Rebaude: ribald, rascal.
Reclaymed: tamed, made gentle; a hawking term.

Recrayed: recreant, cowardly.
Recule: collection of writings.
Refiary: scent.
Remorde: find fault with.
Reporte: refer.
Rew, vb.: have pity.
Rosiar: rose-bush.
Roste: roast.
Rounde: whisper.
Route: crowd.
Rote: root.
Ruddys: ruddy colour in the cheeks.
Rutter, Rutterkyn: gallant (from German reiter, rider).
Ruttyngly: gallantly, dashingly.

S

Sacke: sack, a general name for a class of white wines formerly imported from Spain and the Canaries.
Sadly: soberly.
Sawys: saws, sayings, texts.
Scath: pity.
Shayle: shamble, walk awry.
Shule: shovel.
Skyregalyard: rascal, lewd fellow.
Slo: slay.
Slufferd: slubbered: served in a careless manner.
Smaragd: a type of emerald.
Solfe: solfa, sing.
Sowe (of lead): a large lump.
Stercorry: dung.
Stow: a falconer's cry to bring the hawk to the fist.
Surcudant: presumptuous.
Suspecte: suspicion.
Sysmatike: schismatic, one who promotes division in the Church.

T

Tabers: tabards; short sleeveless coats, still worn by heralds on ceremonial occasions.
Tewly: red; from Toulouse, long famous for silk.
Threte: threaten.
Tote: look upon.
Tranchaunt: trenchant, sharp.
Tratyse: treatise.
Trompe up: proclaim.
Trynall: trinal, threefold.
Tyrid: fastened upon; a hawking term.
Tyrnid: tourneyed.

GLOSSARY

U

Unfayned: displeased.
Untwynde: destroyed, killed.
Utter: away, outside.

V

Vaunteperler: one who is too ready to speak, a pushful person.
Velyarde: dotard.

W

Wache: watch.
Werre: war.

Wesaunt: weasand, throat.
Wheled: wealed.
Whym-wham: a trifling ornament.
Whynnymeg, over in a: the beginning of an old ballad.
Wyght: white.
Whytyng: darling, pretty-one.
Wrythen: twisted.

Y

Yarke: lash with a whip, strike.
Yede: went.
Y-wis: certainly, indeed.

INDEX

INDEX

Erasmus, 2, 9, 12, 18, 106, 131
Erthe upon Erthe, 25

F

Fashions, Skelton's view of Tudor,
   90-1
Ferdinand I, the Emperor, 80
Flodden, Battle of, 80, 118, 119
Foligno, C., 40
Francis I, 80, 81, 82
Froude, J. A., 12
Fuller, Thomas, 3, 21
Furnivall, F. J., 102

G

Gaguin, R., 129
Gairdner, James, 73
Garlande of Laurell, The, 9, 15, 58, 77,
   78, 123-30, 142
Garnesche, Poems against, 8, 10, 65-70,
   103, 117, 121
Genealogia Deorum, 137
Go, pytyous hart, 29
Gower, John, 12, 13, 14, 15, 16, 72,
   125
Greek, study of, 6, 130
Greg, W. W., 76
Guienne, expedition to, 79

H

Hampton Court, 110-1
Harwich, 40, 87, 124
Hawes, Stephen, 27, 35
Hawking, 71, 72, 73, 87-8
Henderson, Philip, 143, 144
Henry VII, 8, 36, 87
— VIII, 9, 11, 12, 16, 18, 20, 66, 69,
   76, 78, 81, 82, 83, 84, 98, 100, 104,
   118, 119, 120, 121
Heresy, 133, 134, 135
Herford, C. H., 36
*Hester, A New Enterlude of Godly
   Queene*, 76
Hoccleve, Thomas, 14, 35, 94
Holbein, Hans, 11
Homer, 2, 125
Horace, 136
Howard, Henry, Earl of Surrey, 123
Hughes, Richard, 143, 144
Humanism, 5, 54, 56, 130-3

I

Islip, John, Abbot of Westminster, 24

J

James I of Scotland, 118, 119
— V of Scotland, 120
James, M. R., 141
Johnson, Samuel, 139

K

Kennedy, Walter, 66
Knolege, aquayntance, resort, 29, 30
Koelbing, A., 36

L

Laureation, Skelton's, 7, 8, 10
Lewis, C. S., 39
Lilly, William, 132
London, 20, 83, 87
Louis XI, 80
— XII, 80
Louvain, University of, 10
Lullay, lullay, 33
Lydgate, John, 12, 13, 14, 15, 17, 30,
   125
Lyrics, mediaeval Latin, 54-5

M

Macaulay, G. C., 72
Magnyfycence, 4, 58, 76-98, 99, 138
Manerly Margery, 33, 143
Manuale Scholarium, The, 131
Marriage, Skelton's alleged, 22
Mass, The, 5
Maximilian I, the Emperor, 79, 80, 84
Mead, W. E., 27
Mediaevalism, Skelton's, 58, 131, 138-9
Medwall, Thomas, 83
Merie Tales of Skelton, 20, 22
Milan, 84
Miroir de l'Omme, 72
Mirry Margaret, 128-9
Moralities, 82, 83, 97
More, Sir Thomas, 135
Morey, Adrian, 32
Mountjoy, Lord, 11
Mullinger, J. B., 134
Monroe, R., 131
Murray, H. M. R., 25
Music, Skelton's Knowledge of, 31,
   32, 68

N

Naylor, A. W., 32
Nelson, William, 9, 20, 24, 99
Nevill, R., 27
Nigramansir, The, 77-8
Nix, Bishop, of Norwich, 21

150

INDEX

INDEX